VOICES OF MODERN GREECE

THE LOCKERT LIBRARY OF POETRY IN TRANSLATION
EDITORIAL ADVISER, JOHN FREDERICK NIMS
For other titles in the Lockert Library see page 203

VOICES OF MODERN GREECE

Selected Poems
by
Cavafy, Sikelianos,
Seferis, Elytis, Gatsos

Translated and edited by
EDMUND KEELEY and PHILIP SHERRARD

Princeton University Press
Princeton, New Jersey

Published by Princeton University Press
Princeton, New Jersey

LCC 81-47282
ISBN 0-691-06473-3
ISBN 0-691-01382-9 pbk

Printed in the United States of America
by Princeton University Press, Princeton, New Jersey

First PRINCETON PAPERBACK printing, 1981

CONTENTS

PREFACE

This selection from the work of five major poets of modern Greece is the crystallization of an undertaking in which we have been engaged for over thirty years. During these years we have published translations of the collected poems of two of the poets here included (C.P. Cavafy and George Seferis), and of a considerable selection from the poetry of a third (Angelos Sikelianos). A selection from the poetry of a fourth (Odysseus Elytis) is about to be published by Viking-Penguin and The Anvil Press, supplementing what has appeared of his work in two previous anthologies, both of which also included work by the fifth (Nikos Gatsos). During the past thirty years, our versions of this poetry have been revised several times, but in particular during the last year, when our translations of Cavafy, Seferis, Sikelianos and Elytis were revised for new editions of the work of each. This being the case, we felt that the time had come for us to go through these new versions and put together a volume that in our judgment does the fullest justice of which we are capable both to our own efforts as translators and to the poets we have translated. In other words, the anthology that we offer here is composed of those translations that seem to us to come over most successfully into English and at the same time to be representative of the best in the poetry of the original poets. We do not mean to imply by this that the selections in our anthology should take the place of the more ample volumes devoted to the individual poets. On the contrary, it is our hope that what we provide here will encourage the reader to turn to those volumes with a view to exploring the work of each poet in greater depth.

We are grateful to the following for granting us permission to publish revised versions of translations which originally appeared under their imprint: Penguin Books Ltd., publishers of *Four Greek Poets*; Princeton University Press and the Hogarth Press, publishers of *C.P. Cavafy: Collected Poems*; Princeton University Press and George Allen and Unwin, publishers of *Angelos Sikelianos: Selected Poems*; Princeton University Press and Jonathan Cape, publishers of *George Seferis: Collected Poems*;

Viking-Penguin and The Anvil Press, publishers of *Odysseus Elytis: Selected Poems;* and George Savidis for his contribution to the notes on the poems of Cavafy.

Katounia, Limni.   E.K.
Summer 1981.   P.S.

CONSTANTINE P. CAVAFY

CHE FECE . . . IL GRAN RIFIUTO*

For some people the day comes
when they have to declare the great Yes
or the great No. It's clear at once who has the Yes
ready within him; and saying it,

he goes from honor to honor, strong in his conviction.
He who refuses does not repent. Asked again,
he'd still say no. Yet that no—the right no—
drags him down all his life.

INTERRUPTION*

Hasty and inexperienced creatures of the moment,
it's we who interrupt the action of the gods.
In the palaces of Eleusis and Phthia
Demeter and Thetis initiate good works
over high flames and heavy smoke.
But Metaneira always bursts in
from the royal quarters, hair loose, terrified,
and Peleus always gets scared and intervenes.

THE WINDOWS

In these dark rooms where I live out empty days,
I wander round and round
trying to find the windows.
It will be a great relief when a window opens.
But the windows aren't there to be found—
or at least I can't find them. And perhaps
it's better if I don't find them.
Perhaps the light will prove another tyranny.
Who knows what new things it will expose?

THERMOPYLAE*

Honor to those who in the life they lead
define and guard a Thermopylae.
Never betraying what is right,
consistent and just in all they do,
but showing pity also, and compassion;
generous when they're rich, and when they're poor,
still generous in small ways,
still helping as much as they can;
always speaking the truth,
yet without hating those who lie.

And even more honor is due to them
when they foresee (as many do foresee)
that Ephialtis will show up in the end,
that the Medes will break through after all.

WAITING FOR THE BARBARIANS

What are we waiting for, assembled in the forum?

    The barbarians are due here today.

Why isn't anything going on in the senate?
Why are the senators sitting there without legislating?

    Because the barbarians are coming today.
    What's the point of senators making laws now?
    Once the barbarians are here, they'll do the legislating.

Why did our emperor get up so early,
and why is he sitting enthroned at the city's main gate,
in state, wearing the crown?

    Because the barbarians are coming today
    and the emperor's waiting to receive their leader.
    He's even got a scroll to give him,
    loaded with titles, with imposing names.

Why have our two consuls and praetors come out today
wearing their embroidered, their scarlet togas?
Why have they put on bracelets with so many amethysts,
rings sparkling with magnificent emeralds?
Why are they carrying elegant canes
beautifully worked in silver and gold?

    Because the barbarians are coming today
    and things like that dazzle the barbarians.

Why don't our distinguished orators turn up as usual
to make their speeches, say what they have to say?

Because the barbarians are coming today
and they're bored by rhetoric and public speaking.

Why this sudden bewilderment, this confusion?
(How serious people's faces have become.)
Why are the streets and squares emptying so rapidly,
everyone going home lost in thought?

Because night has fallen and the barbarians haven't come.
And some of our men just in from the border say
there are no barbarians any longer.

Now what's going to happen to us without barbarians?
They were, those people, a kind of solution.

8

LONGINGS

Like the beautiful bodies of those who died before growing
     old,
sadly shut away in a sumptuous mausoleum,
roses by the head, jasmine at the feet—
so appear the longings that have passed
without being satisfied, not one of them granted
a single night of pleasure, or one of its radiant mornings.

TROJANS

Our efforts are those of men prone to disaster;
our efforts are like those of the Trojans.
We just begin to get somewhere,
begin to gather a little strength,
grow almost bold and hopeful,

when something always comes up to stop us:
Achilles leaps out of the trench in front of us
and terrifies us with his violent shouting.

Our efforts are like those of the Trojans.
We think we'll change our luck
by being resolute and daring,
so we move outside ready to fight.

But when the big crisis comes,
our boldness and resolution vanish;
our spirit falters, paralyzed,
and we scurry around the walls
trying to save ourselves by running away.

Yet we're sure to fail. Up there,
high on the walls, the dirge has already begun.
They're mourning the memory, the aura of our days.
Priam and Hecuba* mourn for us bitterly.

HIDDEN THINGS

From all I did and all I said
let no one try to find out who I was.
An obstacle was there distorting
the actions and the manner of my life.
An obstacle was often there
to stop me when I'd begin to speak.
From my most unnoticed actions,
my most veiled writing—
from these alone will I be understood.
But maybe it isn't worth so much concern,
so much effort to discover who I really am.
Later, in a more perfect society,
someone else made just like me
is certain to appear and act freely.

THE FOOTSTEPS

Eagles of coral
adorn the ebony bed
where Nero* lies fast asleep—
callous, happy, peaceful,
in the prime of his body's strength,
in the fine vigor of youth.

But in the alabaster hall that holds
the ancient shrine of the Aenobarbi
how restless the household deities!
The little gods tremble
and try to hide their insignificant bodies.
They've heard a terrible sound,
a deadly sound coming up the stairs,
iron footsteps that shake the staircase;
and, faint with fear, the miserable Lares
scramble to the back of the shrine,
shoving each other and stumbling,
one little god falling over another,
because they know what kind of sound that is,
know by now the footsteps of the Furies.

12

THE CITY

You said: "I'll go to another country, go to another shore,
find another city better than this one.
Whatever I try to do is fated to turn out wrong
and my heart lies buried as though it were something dead.
How long can I let my mind moulder in this place?
Wherever I turn, wherever I look,
I see the black ruins of my life, here,
where I've spent so many years, wasted them, destroyed them
        totally."

You won't find a new country, won't find another shore.
This city will always pursue you.
You'll walk the same streets, grow old
in the same neighborhoods, turn grey in these same houses.
You'll always end up in this city. Don't hope for things
        elsewhere:
there's no ship for you, there's no road.
Now that you've wasted your life here, in this small corner,
you've destroyed it everywhere in the world.

THE SATRAPY*

Too bad that, cut out as you are
for grand and noble acts,
this unfair fate of yours
never helps you out, always prevents your success;
that cheap habits get in your way,
pettiness, or indifference.
And how terrible the day you give in
(the day you let go and give in)
and take the road for Susa
to find King Artaxerxes,
who, propitiously, gives you a place at his court
and offers you satrapies and things like that—
things you don't want at all,
though, in despair, you accept them just the same.
You're longing for something else, aching for other things:
praise from the Demos and the Sophists,
that hard-won, that priceless acclaim—
the Agora, the Theatre, the Crowns of Laurel.
You can't get any of these from Artaxerxes,
you'll never find any of these in the satrapy,
and without them, what kind of life will you live?

14

THE IDES OF MARCH*

My soul, guard against pomp and glory.
And if you can't curb your ambitions,
at least pursue them hesitantly, cautiously.
And the higher you go,
the more searching and careful you need to be.

And when you reach your summit, Caesar at last—
when you assume the role of someone that famous—
then be specially careful as you go out into the street,
a conspicuous man of power with your retinue;
and should a certain Artemidoros
come up to you out of the crowd, bringing a letter,
and say hurriedly: "Read this at once.
There are important things in it concerning you,"
be sure to stop; be sure to postpone
all talk or business; be sure to brush off
all those who salute and bow to you
(they can be seen later); let even
the Senate itself wait—and find out immediately
what important message Artemidoros has for you.

THE GOD ABANDONS ANTONY *

When suddenly at midnight you hear
an invisible procession going by
with exquisite music, voices,
don't mourn your luck that's failing now,
work gone wrong, your plans
all proving deceptive—don't mourn them uselessly:
as one long prepared, and full of courage,
say goodbye to her, to Alexandria who is leaving.
Above all, don't fool yourself, don't say
it was a dream, your ears deceived you:
don't degrade yourself with empty hopes like these.
As one long prepared, and full of courage,
as is right for you who were given this kind of city,
go firmly to the window
and listen with deep emotion,
but not with the whining, the pleas of a coward;
listen—your final pleasure—to the voices,
to the exquisite music of that strange procession,
and say goodbye to her, to the Alexandria you are losing.

IONIC

That we've broken their statues,
that we've driven them out of their temples,
doesn't mean at all that the gods are dead.
O land of Ionia, they're still in love with you,
their souls still keep your memory.
When an August dawn wakes over you,
your atmosphere is potent with their life,
and sometimes a young ethereal figure,
indistinct, in rapid flight,
wings across your hills.

ITHAKA

As you set out for Ithaka
hope the journey may be long,
full of adventure, full of discovery.
Laistrygonians, Cyclops,*
angry Poseidon—don't be afraid of them:
you'll never find things like that on your way
as long as you keep your thoughts raised high,
as long as a rare excitement
stirs your spirit and your body.
Laistrygonians, Cyclops,
wild Poseidon—you won't encounter them
unless you bring them along inside your soul,
unless your soul sets them up in front of you.

Hope the journey may be long.
May there be many a summer morning
when with what pleasure, what joy,
you enter harbors you're seeing for the first time;
may you stop at Phoenician trading stations
to buy fine things,
mother of pearl and coral, amber and ebony,
sensual perfume of every kind—
as many sensual perfumes as you can;
and may you visit many Egyptian cities
to learn, and go on learning, from their scholars.

Keep Ithaka always in your mind.
Arriving there is what you're destined for.
But don't hurry the journey at all.
Better if it lasts for years,
so you're old by the time you reach the island,

wealthy with all you've gained on the way,
not expecting Ithaka to make you rich.

Ithaka gave you the marvellous journey.
Without her you wouldn't have set out.
She has nothing left to give you now.

And if you find her poor, Ithaka won't have fooled you.
Wise as you will have become, so full of experience,
you'll have understood by then what these Ithakas mean.

PHILHELLENE

Make sure the engraving is done skillfully.
The expression serious, majestic.
The diadem preferably somewhat narrow:
I don't like that broad kind the Parthians wear.
The inscription, as usual, in Greek:
nothing excessive or pompous—
we don't want the proconsul to take it the wrong way;
he's always smelling things out and reporting back to Rome—
but of course giving me due honor.
Something very special on the other side:
perhaps a discus-thrower, young, good-looking.
Above all I urge you to see to it
(Sithaspis, for God's sake don't let them forget)
that after "King" and "Savior,"
they add "Philhellene" in elegant characters.
Now don't try to be clever
with your "where are the Greeks?" and "what Hellenism
here behind Zagros, out beyond Phraata?"*
Since so many others more barbarian than ourselves
choose to inscribe it, we'll inscribe it too.
And besides, don't forget that sometimes
sophists do come to us from Syria,
and versifiers, and other triflers of that kind.
So we are not, I think, un-Hellenized.

ALEXANDRIAN KINGS*

The Alexandrians turned out in force
to see Cleopatra's children,
Kaisarion and his little brothers,
Alexander and Ptolemy,
who'd been taken out to the Gymnasium for the first time,
to be proclaimed kings there
before a brilliant array of soldiers.

Alexander: they declared him
king of Armenia, Media, and the Parthians.
Ptolemy: they declared him
king of Cilicia, Syria, and Phoenicia.
Kaisarion was standing in front of the others,
dressed in pink silk,
on his chest a bunch of hyacinths,
his belt a double row of amethysts and sapphires,
his shoes tied with white ribbons
prinked with rose-colored pearls.
They declared him greater than his brothers,
they declared him King of Kings.

The Alexandrians knew of course
that this was all just words, all theatre.

But the day was warm and poetic,
the sky a pale blue,
the Alexandrian Gymnasium
a complete artistic triumph,
the courtiers wonderfully sumptuous,
Kaisarion all grace and beauty
(Cleopatra's son, blood of the Lagids);
and the Alexandrians thronged to the festival

full of enthusiasm, and shouted acclamations
in Greek, and Egyptian, and some in Hebrew,
charmed by the lovely spectacle—
though they knew of course what all this was worth,
what empty words they really were, these kingships.

AS MUCH AS YOU CAN

Even if you can't shape your life the way you want,
at least try as much as you can
not to degrade it
by too much contact with the world,
by too much activity and talk.

Do not degrade it by dragging it along,
taking it around and exposing it so often
to the daily silliness
of social events and parties,
until it comes to seem a boring hanger-on.

EXILES*

It goes on being Alexandria still. Just walk a bit
along the straight road that ends at the Hippodrome
and you'll see palaces and monuments that will amaze you.
Whatever war-damage it's suffered,
however much smaller it's become,
it's still a wonderful city.
And then, what with excursions and books
and various kinds of study, time does go by.
In the evenings we meet on the sea front,
the five of us (all, naturally, under fictitious names)
and some of the few other Greeks
still left in the city.
Sometimes we discuss church affairs
(the people here seem to lean toward Rome)
and sometimes literature.
The other day we read some lines by Nonnos:
what imagery, what rhythm, what diction and harmony!
All enthusiasm, how we admired the Panopolitan.
So the days go by, and our stay here
isn't unpleasant because, naturally,
it's not going to last forever.
We've had good news: if something doesn't come
of what's now afoot in Smyrna,
then in April our friends are sure to move from Epiros,
so one way or another our plans are definitely working out,
and we'll easily overthrow Basil.
And when we do, at last our turn will come.

24

THEODOTOS *

If you are one of the truly elect,
be careful how you attain your eminence.
However much you're acclaimed, however much
the cities praise the great things you've done
in Italy and Thessaly,
whatever honors
your admirers decree for you in Rome,
your elation, your triumph won't last,
nor will you feel yourself so superior—
superior is the last thing you'll feel—
when Theodotos brings you, in Alexandria,
on a blood-stained tray,
miserable Pompey's head.

And don't be too sure that in your life—
restricted, regulated, prosaic—
spectacular and horrible things like that don't happen.
Maybe this very moment Theodotos—
bodiless, invisible—
enters some neighbor's tidy house
carrying an equally repulsive head.

FOR AMMONIS, WHO DIED AT 29, IN 610

Raphael, they're asking you to write a few lines
as an epitaph for the poet Ammonis:
something very tasteful and polished. You can do it,
you're the one to write something suitable
for the poet Ammonis, our Ammonis.

Of course you'll speak about his poems—
but say something too about his beauty,
about that subtle beauty we loved.

Your Greek is always elegant and musical.
But we want all your craftsmanship now.
Our sorrow and our love move into a foreign language.
Pour your Egyptian feeling into the Greek you use.

Raphael, your verses, you know, should be written
so they contain something of our life within them,
so the rhythm, so every phrase clearly shows
that an Alexandrian is writing about an Alexandrian.

HALF AN HOUR

I never had you nor, I suppose,
will I ever have you. A few words, an approach,
as in the bar yesterday—nothing more.
It's sad, I admit. But we who serve Art,
sometimes with the mind's intensity
can create pleasure that seems almost physical—
but of course only for a short time.
That's how in the bar yesterday—
mercifully helped by alcohol—
I had half an hour that was totally erotic.
And I think you understood this
and stayed slightly longer on purpose.
That was very necessary.
Because with all the imagination,
all the magic alcohol,
I needed to see your lips as well,
needed your body near me.

ONE OF THEIR GODS

When one of them moved through the center of Selefkia*
just as it was getting dark—
moved like a young man, tall, extremely handsome,
the joy of being immortal in his eyes,
his hair black and perfumed—
the people going by would gaze at him,
and one would ask the other if he knew him,
if he was a Greek from Syria, or a stranger.
But some who looked more carefully
would understand and step aside;
and as he disappeared under the arcades,
among the shadows and the evening lights,
going toward the quarter that lives
only at night, with orgies and debauchery,
with every kind of intoxication and desire,
they would wonder which of Them it could be,
and for what suspicious pleasure
he'd come down into the streets of Selefkia
from the August Celestial Mansions.

IN THE EVENING

It wouldn't have lasted long anyway—
the experience of years makes that clear.
But Fate did put an end to it a bit abruptly.
It was soon over, that wonderful life.
Yet how strong the scents were,
what a magnificent bed we lay in,
what pleasures we gave our bodies.

An echo from my days of indulgence,
an echo from those days came back to me,
something of the fire of the young life we shared:
I picked up a letter again,
read it over and over till the light faded.

Then, sad, I went out to the balcony,
went out to change my thoughts at least by seeing
something of this city I love,
a little movement in the streets, in the shops.

KAISARION*

Partly to verify the facts of a certain period,
partly to kill an hour or two,
last night I picked up and read
a volume of inscriptions about the Ptolemies.
The lavish praise and flattery are much the same
for each of them. All are brilliant,
glorious, mighty, benevolent;
everything they undertake is full of wisdom.
As for the women of their line, the Berenices and Cleopatras,
they too, all of them, are marvellous.

When I'd found the facts I wanted
I would have put the book away, but a brief
insignificant mention of King Kaisarion
suddenly caught my eye . . .

There you stood with your indefinable charm.
Because so little
is known about you from history,
I could fashion you more freely in my mind.
I made you good-looking and sensitive.
My art gives your face
a dreamy, appealing beauty.
And so completely did I imagine you
that late last night,
as my lamp went out—I let it go out on purpose—
I thought you came into my room,
it seemed you stood there in front of me looking just as you
        would have
in conquered Alexandria,
pale and weary, ideal in your grief,
still hoping they might take pity on you,
those scum who whispered: "Too many Caesars."

BODY, REMEMBER...

Body, remember not only how much you were loved,
not only the beds you lay on,
but also those desires glowing openly
in eyes that looked at you,
trembling for you in voices—
only some chance obstacle frustrated them.
Now that it's all finally in the past,
it seems almost as if you gave yourself
to those desires too—how they glowed,
remember, in eyes that looked at you,
remember, body, how they trembled for you in those voices.

SINCE NINE O'CLOCK

Half past twelve. Time's gone by quickly
since nine o'clock when I lit the lamp
and sat down here. I've been sitting without reading,
without speaking. Completely alone in the house,
whom could I talk to?

Since nine o'clock when I lit the lamp
the shade of my young body
has been haunting me, reminding me
of shut scented rooms,
of past passion—what daring passion.
And it's also brought back to me
streets now unrecognizable,
bustling night clubs now closed,
theatres and cafés no longer there.

The shade of my young body
also brought back the things that make us sad:
family grief, separation,
the feelings of my own people,
of the dead so little recognized.

Half past twelve: how the time has gone by.
Half past twelve: how the years have gone by.

THE AFTERNOON SUN

This room, how well I know it.
Now they're renting it, and the one next to it,
as offices. The whole house has become
an office building for agents, businessmen, companies.

This room, how familiar it is.

The couch was here, near the door,
a Turkish carpet in front of it.
Close by, the shelf with two yellow vases.
On the right—no, opposite—a wardrobe with a mirror.
In the middle the table where he wrote,
and the three big wicker chairs.
Beside the window the bed
where we made love so many times.

They must still be around somewhere, those old things.

Beside the window the bed;
the afternoon sun used to touch half of it.

. . . One afternoon at four o'clock we separated
for a week only . . . And then—
that week became forever.

DAREIOS*

Phernazis the poet is at work
on the crucial part of his epic:
how Dareios, son of Hystaspis,
took over the Persian kingdom.
(It's from him, Dareios, that our glorious king,
Mithridatis, Dionysos and Evpator, descends.)
But this calls for serious thought; Phernazis has to analyze
the feelings Dareios must have had:
arrogance, perhaps, and intoxication? No—more likely
a certain insight into the vanities of greatness.
The poet thinks deeply about the question.

But his servant, rushing in,
cuts him short to announce very important news:
the war with the Romans has begun;
most of our army has crossed the borders.

The poet is dumbfounded. What a disaster!
How can our glorious king,
Mithridatis, Dionysos and Evpator,
bother about Greek poems now?
In the middle of a war—just think, Greek poems!

Phernazis gets all worked up. What a bad break!
Just when he was sure to distinguish himself
with his *Dareios*, sure to make
his envious critics shut up once and for all.
What a setback, terrible setback to his plans.

And if it's only a setback, that wouldn't be too bad.
But can we really consider ourselves safe in Amisos?
The town isn't very well fortified,

and the Romans are the most awful enemies.
Are we, Cappadocians, really a match for them?
Is it conceivable?
Are we to compete with the legions?
Great gods, protectors of Asia, help us.

But through all his nervousness, all the turmoil,
the poetic idea comes and goes insistently:
arrogance and intoxication—that's the most likely, of course:
arrogance and intoxication are what Dareios must have felt.

FROM THE SCHOOL OF THE RENOWNED
PHILOSOPHER

For two years he studied with Ammonios Sakkas,*
but he was bored by both philosophy and Sakkas.

Then he went into politics.
But he gave that up. The Prefect was an idiot,
and those around him solemn, officious nitwits:
their Greek—poor fools—barbaric.

After that he became
vaguely curious about the Church: to be baptized
and pass as a Christian. But he soon
let that one drop: it would certainly have caused a row
with his parents, ostentatious pagans,
and right away they would have cut off—
something too horrible to contemplate—
their extremely generous allowance.

But he had to do something. He began to haunt
the corrupt houses of Alexandria,
every secret den of debauchery.

Here he was fortunate:
he'd been given an extremely handsome figure,
and he enjoyed the divine gift.

His looks would last
at least another ten years. And after that?
Perhaps he'll go back to Sakkas.
Or if the old man has died meanwhile,
he'll find another philosopher or sophist:
there's always someone suitable around.

Or in the end he might possibly return
even to politics—commendably remembering
the traditions of his family,
duty toward the country,
and other resonant banalities of that kind.

IN A TOWNSHIP OF ASIA MINOR

The news from Actium, about the outcome of the sea-battle,
was of course unexpected.
But there's no need for us to draw up a new proclamation.
The name's the only thing that has to be changed.
There, in the concluding lines, instead of: "Having freed the
        Romans
from Octavius, that disaster,
that parody of a Caesar,"
we'll substitute: "Having freed the Romans
from Antony, that disaster,..."
The whole text fits very nicely.

"To the most glorious victor,
matchless in his military ventures,
prodigious in his political operations,
on whose behalf the township ardently wished
for Antony's triumph,..."
here, as we said, the substitution: "for Octavius' triumph,
regarding it Zeus' finest gift—
to this mighty protector of the Greeks,
who graciously honors Greek customs,
who is beloved in every Greek domain,
who clearly deserves exalted praise,
and whose exploits should be recorded at length
in the Greek language, in both verse and prose,
in the *Greek language*, the vehicle of fame,"
et cetera, et cetera. It all fits brilliantly.

IN SPARTA *

He didn't know, King Kleomenis, he didn't dare—
he just didn't know how to tell his mother
a thing like that: Ptolemy's demand,
to guarantee their treaty, that she too go to Egypt
and be held there as a hostage—
a very humiliating, indecorous thing.
And he would be about to speak yet always hesitate,
would start to tell her yet always stop.

But the magnificent woman understood him
(she'd already heard some rumors about it)
and she encouraged him to get it out.
And she laughed, saying of course she'd go,
happy even that in her old age
she could be useful to Sparta still.

As for the humiliation—that didn't touch her at all.
Of course an upstart like the Lagid
couldn't possibly comprehend the Spartan spirit;
so his demand couldn't in fact humiliate
a Royal Lady like herself:
mother of a Spartan king.

IN A LARGE GREEK COLONY, 200 B.C.

That things in the Colony aren't what they should be
no one can doubt any longer,
and though in spite of everything we do move forward,
maybe—as more than a few believe—the time has come
to bring in a Political Reformer.

But here's the problem, here's the rub:
they make a tremendous fuss
about everything, these Reformers.
(What a relief it would be
if they were never needed.) They probe everywhere,
question the smallest detail,
and right away think up radical changes
that demand immediate execution.

Also, they have a liking for sacrifice:
Get rid of that property;
your owning it is risky:
properties like those are what ruin colonies.
Get rid of that income,
and the other connected with it,
and this third, as a natural consequence:
they are substantial, but it can't be helped—
the responsibility they create is damaging.

And as they proceed with their investigation,
they find an endless number of useless things to eliminate—
things that are, however, difficult to get rid of.

And when, all being well, they finish the job,
every detail now diagnosed and sliced away,
and they retire (also taking the wages due to them),

40

it's a wonder anything's left at all
after such surgical efficiency.

Perhaps the moment hasn't arrived yet.
Let's not be too hasty: haste is a dangerous thing.
Untimely measures bring repentance.
Certainly, and unhappily, many things in the Colony are absurd.
But is there anything human without some fault?
And after all, you see, we do move forward.

41

A PRINCE FROM WESTERN LIBYA

Aristomenis, son of Menelaos,
the Prince from Western Libya,
was generally liked in Alexandria
during the ten days he spent there.
In keeping with his name, his dress was also suitably Greek.
He received honors gladly,
but he didn't solicit them; he was unassuming.
He bought Greek books,
especially history and philosophy.
Above all he was a man of few words.
It got around that he must be a profound thinker,
and men like that naturally don't speak very much.

He wasn't a profound thinker or anything at all—
just a piddling, laughable man.
He assumed a Greek name, dressed like the Greeks,
learned to behave more or less like a Greek;
and all the time he was terrified he'd spoil
his reasonably good image
by coming out with barbaric howlers in Greek
and the Alexandrians, in their usual way,
would start to make fun of him, vile people that they are.

This was why he limited himself to a few words,
terribly careful of his syntax and pronunciation;
and he was driven almost out of his mind, having
so much talk bottled up inside him.

MYRIS: ALEXANDRIA, A.D. 340

When I heard the terrible news, that Myris was dead,
I went to his house, although I avoid
going to the houses of Christians,
especially during times of mourning or festivity.

I stood in the corridor. I didn't want
to go further inside because I noticed
that the relatives of the deceased looked at me
with obvious surprise and displeasure.

They had him in a large room
and from the corner where I stood
I could catch a glimpse of it: all precious carpets,
and vessels in silver and gold.

I stood and wept in a corner of the corridor.
And I thought how our parties and excursions
wouldn't be worthwhile now without Myris;
and I thought how I'd no longer see him
at our wonderfully indecent night-long sessions
enjoying himself, laughing, and reciting verses
with his perfect feel for Greek rhythm;
and I thought how I'd lost forever
his beauty, lost forever
the young man I'd worshipped so passionately.

Some old women close to me were talking with lowered voices
about the last day he lived:
the name of Christ constantly on his lips,
his hand holding a cross.
Then four Christian priests
came into the room, and said prayers

fervently, and orisons to Jesus,
or to Mary (I'm not very familiar with their religion).

We'd known of course that Myris was a Christian,
known it from the very start,
when he first joined our group the year before last.

But he lived exactly as we did:
more devoted to pleasure than all of us,
he scattered his money lavishly on amusements.
Not caring what anyone thought of him,
he threw himself eagerly into night-time scuffles
when our group happened to clash
with some rival group in the street.
He never spoke about his religion.
And once we even told him
that we'd take him with us to the Serapeion.*
But—I remember now—
he didn't seem to like this joke of ours.
And yes, now I recall two other incidents.
When we made libations to Poseidon,
he drew himself back from our circle and looked elsewhere.
And when one of us in his fervor said:
"May all of us be favored and protected
by the great, the sublime Apollo" —
Myris, unheard by the others, whispered: "Not counting me."

The Christian priests were praying loudly
for the young man's soul.
I noticed with how much diligence,
how much intense concern
for the forms of their religion, they were preparing
everything for the Christian funeral.
And suddenly an odd sensation took hold of me:
indefinably I felt

44

as if Myris were going from me;
I felt that he, a Christian, was united
with his own people and that I was becoming
a stranger, a total stranger. I even felt
a doubt come over me: that I'd been deceived by my passion
and had always been a stranger to him.
I rushed out of their horrible house,
rushed away before my memory of Myris
could be captured, could be perverted by their Christianity.

TO HAVE TAKEN THE TROUBLE

I'm practically broke and homeless.
This fatal city, Antioch,
has devoured all my money:
this fatal city with its extravagant life.

But I'm young and in excellent health.
Prodigious master of Greek,
I know Aristotle and Plato through and through,
poets, orators, or anyone else you could mention.
I have some idea about military matters
and friends among the senior mercenaries.
I also have a foot in the administrative world;
I spent six months in Alexandria last year:
I know (and this is useful) something about what goes on
        there—
the scheming of Kakergetis,* his dirty deals, and the rest of it.

So I consider myself completely qualified
to serve this country,
my beloved fatherland, Syria.

Whatever job they give me,
I'll try to be useful to the country. That's what I intend.
But if they frustrate me with their maneuvers—
we know them, those smart operators: no need to say more
        here—
if they frustrate me, it's not my fault.

I'll approach Zabinas first,
and if that idiot doesn't appreciate me,
I'll go to his rival, Grypos.

46

And if that imbecile doesn't appoint me,
I'll go straight to Hyrkanos.

One of the three will want me anyway.

And my conscience is quiet
about my not caring which one I choose:
the three of them are equally bad for Syria.

But, a ruined man, it's not my fault.
I'm only trying, poor devil, to make ends meet.
The almighty gods ought to have taken the trouble
to create a fourth, a decent man.
I would gladly have gone along with him.

IN THE YEAR 200 B.C.

"Alexander, son of Philip, and the Greeks except the
        Lacedaimonians ..."*

We can very well imagine
how completely indifferent the Spartans would have been
to this inscription. "Except the Lacedaimonians"—
naturally. The Spartans weren't to be led
and ordered around
like precious servants. Besides,
they wouldn't have thought a pan-Hellenic expedition
without a Spartan king in command
was to be taken very seriously.
Of course, then, "except the Lacedaimonians."

That's certainly one point of view. Quite understandable.

So, "except the Lacedaimonians" at Granikos,
then at Issus, then in the decisive battle
where the terrible army
the Persians mustered at Arbela was wiped out:
it set out for victory from Arbela, and was wiped out.

And from this marvellous pan-Hellenic expedition,
triumphant, brilliant in every way,
celebrated on all sides, glorified
as no other has ever been glorified,
incomparable, we emerged:
the great new Hellenic world.

We the Alexandrians, the Antiochians,
the Selefkians, and the countless
other Greeks of Egypt and Syria,

and those in Media, and Persia, and all the rest:
with our far-flung supremacy,
our flexible policy of judicious integration,
and our Common Greek Language
which we carried as far as Bactria, as far as the Indians.

How can one talk about Lacedaimonians after that!

ON THE OUTSKIRTS OF ANTIOCH*

We in Antioch were astonished when we heard
what Julian was up to now.

Apollo had made things clear to him at Daphni:
he didn't want to give an oracle (as though we cared!),
he didn't intend to speak prophetically
unless his temple at Daphni was purified first.
The nearby dead, he declared, got on his nerves.

There are many tombs at Daphni.
One of those buried there
was the triumphant and holy martyr Vavylas,
wonder and glory of our church.

It was him the false god hinted at, him he feared.
As long as he felt him near he didn't dare
pronounce his oracle: not a murmur.
(The false gods are terrified of our martyrs.)

Unholy Julian got worked up,
lost his temper and shouted: "Raise him, carry him out,
take him away immediately, this Vavylas.
You there, do you hear? He gets on Apollo's nerves.
Grab him, raise him at once,
dig him out, take him wherever you want,
take him away, throw him out. This isn't a joke.
Apollo said the temple has to be purified."

We took it, the holy relic, and carried it elsewhere.
We took it, we carried it in love and in honor.

And hasn't the temple done brilliantly since!
In no time at all a colossal fire broke out,
a terrible fire,
and both the temple and Apollo burned to the ground.

Ashes the idol: dirt to be swept away.

Julian blew up, and he spread it around—
what else could he do?—that we, the Christians,
had set the fire. Let him say so.
It hasn't been proved. Let him say so.
The essential thing is: he blew up.

ANGELOS SIKELIANOS

SPARTA *

"A long time now I've lain in wait for you;
my eye singled you out from all the others
as though you lived among them like a star;
your grace and beauty gratify my heart.

Listen—let me grip your hand firmly:
youth is tamed that way, like a stallion—
for a single night, in my own bed,
you will be partner to my wife!

Go. She is slim-waisted, a woman
pledged to beauty as tall Helen was.
Go, fill her with your generous seed.

Take her in your powerful embrace
for one night only, and in Sparta's eyes,
through a worthy son, exalt my dry old age."

DORIC

Her hair curled in at the nape of her neck
like the Doric Apollo's hair, she kept
her limbs frozen on the narrow bed
in a heavy, indissoluble cloud.

Artemis fired all her arrows at her.
And though she soon would cease to be a virgin,
still her virgin legs, like a cold honeycomb,
sealed in her sensual joy.

As if in combat in the ring,
he knelt, his body oiled with myrrh,
to press her as a wrestler might.

And though he breached her out-thrust arms,
it was some time before they locked their lips,
cried out as one, and in their sweat embraced . . .

56

ON ACROCORINTH*

The sun set over Acrocorinth
burning the rock red. From the sea
a fragrant smell of seaweed now began
to intoxicate my slender stallion.

Foam on the bit, the white of his eye
bared fully, he struggled to break
my grip, tight on his reins,
to leap free into open space.

Was it the hour? The rich odors?
Was it the sea's deep saltiness?
The forest's breathing far away?

O had the etesian wind held strong
a little longer, I would have gripped
the reins and flanks of mythic Pegasus!*

CAIQUE

Caique in the wind's center.
sails hauled in bow-taut,
tiller swinging into the final tack
against the bare blue mountains.

And the heaven-coursing howl that swamped
rigging, moorings in the stern, the yard
—dolphins in pursuit all the way—
strummed her over the waves: an upright lyre.

Double-headed axe, the keel carved.
And the wake's foam, twinned as lilies,
rattled the sistrum of the water's falling.

Then with a sudden "bear off"
—sun at its zenith—the caique found
Salona harbor in the noon's nor'wester.*

THE FIRST RAIN

We leaned out of the window.
Everything around us
was one with our soul.
Sulphur-pale, the clouds
darkened the fields, the vines;
wind moaned in the trees
with a secret turbulence,
and the quick swallow went
breasting across the grass.
Suddenly the thunder broke,
the wellhead broke,
and dancing came the rain.
Dust leaped into the air.
We, our nostrils quivering,
opened our lips to drink
the earth's heavy smell,
to let it like a spring
water us deep inside
(the rain had already wet
our thirsting faces,
like the olive and the mullein).
And shoulder touching shoulder,
we asked: "What smell is this
that cuts the air like a bee?
From balsam, pine-cone, acanthus,
from osier or thyme?"
So many the scents that, breathing out,
I became a lyre caressed
by the breath's profusion.
Sweetness filled my palate;
and as our eyes met again
all my blood sang out.

I bent down to the vine,
its leaves shaking, to drink
its honey and its flower;
and—my thoughts like heavy grapes,
bramble-thick my breath—
I could not, as I breathed,
choose among the scents,
but culled them all, and drank them
as one drinks joy or sorrow
suddenly sent by fate;
I drank them all,
and when I touched your waist,
my blood became a nightingale,
became like the running waters.

PAN

Over rocks on the deserted shore, over the burning heat
        of harsh pebbles,
beside the emerald waves, noon, like a fountain,
        rose shimmering.

Salamis a blue trireme deep in the sea,*
        in spring's spindrift;
the pines and mastic trees of Kineta a deep breath*
        I drew inside me.

The sea burst into foam and, beaten by the wind,
        shattered white,
and a flock of goats, countless, iron-gray, plummeted headlong
        down the hill.

With two harsh whistles, fingers pressing
        his curled tongue,
the goatherd huddled them on the shore,
        the whole five hundred.

They gathered in close, crowding the brush
        and wild thyme,
and as they gathered, a drowsiness seized
        both goats and man.

And then, over the shore's stones and the goats' swelter,
        dead silence;
and between their horns, as from a tripod, the sun's quick heat
        shimmered upward.

Then we saw the herd's lord and master, the he-goat,
        rise alone

61

and move off, his tread slow and heavy,
        towards a rock

wedged into the sea to shape a perfect look-out point;
        there he stopped,
on the very edge where spray dissolves,
        and leaning motionless,

upper lip pulled back so that his teeth shone,
        he stood
huge, erect, smelling the white-crested sea
        until sunset.

THALERO*

Glowing, festive, warm, the moon looked down
 over the vineyards
while the sun still scorched the bushes, setting
 in total stillness.

The heavy grass up on the windless height sweated
 its pungent sap,
and among the new-leaved vines that climbed
 the terraced slope

the buntings fluttered and called, the robins
 hovered on the banks,
and the heat spread a fine filmy veil across
 the moon's face.

On the path between the wheat fields three oxen,
 one behind the other,
ascended the mountain slope, their pendant
 dewlaps swaying.

The slender hound, his muzzle to the earth
 in the quiet evening,
leaped from rock to rock, searching
 for my tracks.

And at the house ahead, beneath the unripe vine,
 a ready table
waited for me, a lamp hung out in front of it—
 the evening star.

There the master's daughter brought me honeycomb, cold water,
 country bread;

her strength had engraved around her rock-like throat a circle
        like a dove's ring;

and her look, like the evening light, disclosed virginity's
        lucid flame,
and through the tight dress that covered her firm breasts the
    nipples
        stood out boldly.

Her hair was plaited in two braids
        above her forehead—
braids like the cables of a ship, too thick
        for my hand's grip.

The dog, exhausted now from the steep footpaths,
        stood there panting,
and, motionless, stared into my eyes,
        waiting for a crust.

There, as I heard the nightingale and ate fruit from the dish
        in front of me,
I had the taste of wheat, of song and honey
        deep on the palate.

As in a glass hive my soul moved inside me,
        a joyful bee-swarm
that, secretly increasing, seeks to release into the trees
        its grapelike cluster.

And I felt the earth was crystal beneath my feet,
        the soil transparent,
for the strong and peaceful bodies of tall plane trees
        rose up around me.

There the old wine was opened for me, smelling rich
        in the wooden jar,
as mountain scents when the cool night dew
        falls on the bushes.

Glowing, festive, warm, there my heart consented
        to repose for a while
in sheets made fragrant by herbs, azure
        by washing blue.

THE MOTHER OF DANTE*

In her sleep, as dawn began to break,
        it seemed that Florence had emptied
and that she was alone, far from friends,
        slowly wandering the streets.

Wearing her silk bridal gown
        and her lily-white veils
she roamed through known crossroads, and in her dream
        she imagined the roads new.

And in the hills washed by spring's dawn mist,
        like the distant sound of bees,
the belfries tolled their slow dead ring
        at secluded country chapels.

Suddenly she found herself inside a garden,
        in the white air, a garden
wearing bridal dress, with bitter-orange and apple trees
        stretching into the distance.

And as the fragrance drew her on it seemed
        a laurel tree approached,
and in it, rising step by step,
        a peacock climbed.

The peacock bent its neck from branch to branch,
        the branches rich with berrries,
and sometimes ate and sometimes plucked the fruit
        to throw it to the ground.

And she, against her will, held out her embroidered apron
        in the shade, enraptured,

and soon she felt the weight of it in front,
      heavy with laurel berries.

She rested this way a moment from her dawn's labor
      in the coolness of a cloud;
and round the bed her women friends waited
      to receive the coming child . . .

BECAUSE I DEEPLY PRAISED

Because I deeply praised and trusted earth
and did not spread my secret wings in flight
but rooted in the stillness all my mind,
the spring again has risen to my thirst,
the dancing spring of life, my own joy's spring.

Because I never questioned how and when
but plunged my thought into each passing hour
as though its boundless goal lay hidden there,
no matter if I live in calm or storm,
the rounded moment shimmers in my mind,
the fruit falls from the sky, falls deep inside me.

Because I did not say: "here life starts, here ends,"
but "days of rain bring on a richer light
and earthquakes give the world a firmer base,
for secret is earth's live creative pulse,"
all fleeting things dissolve away like clouds,
great Death itself has now become my kin.

DAEDALUS*

The fate of Icarus could have been no other
than to fly and to perish.... Because when he put on
freedom's awe-inspiring wings, their equipoise the art
of his great father, it was youth alone
that flung his body into danger, even if
he also failed, perhaps, to find their secret balance.

And men untried by suffering were shaken,
women were shaken, when over the huge sea
they saw an adolescent body upright
thresh the winds like a gull, and suddenly
plunge from sight.
                              And then it was as if
they saw the whole sea like an endless teardrop,
a deep lament which, telling and retelling
the young boy's name, took from that name
soul and meaning and its own true sound.

But if a man who from his earliest years
has said that the heavens and the earth are one,
that his own thought is the world's hearth and center,
and that the earth may mingle with the stars
as a field's subsoil with its topsoil, so that the heavens too
may bring forth wheat;
                              if a man who has seen
that all human beings, their souls and their works,
lie in the grave's shadow, and has resolved
to set them free as already he has set free
the arms and legs of statues, so that they might walk
with their own motion along the paths of light;
who, just as he has ribbed the celestial ship
with the strong trunks of trees, has loaded it

not with ivory or amber or with gold
but with all the Heroes, chosen one by one
for the deathless voyages of myth;
                                    if a man
shut up in a prison built with his own hands—
as the caterpillar on its own will weave the tomb
in which it shuts itself, seeking through death
wholly to change its nature—if such a man
deep in the Labyrinth has dreamed that wings
have sprouted on his shoulders, and step by step
his waking mind has wrestled with the dream
until he has mastered it;
                                    and though his body
is spent from all that strain, when he has seen
the dull crowd around him suddenly try to treat
his awe-inspiring Art, whose end was fixed in God,
as the mere bauble of an idle mind,
has girded those wings like armor, and slowly
has raised himself, has climbed among the winds,
reaping them peacefully as with his scythe
the reaper cuts in front of him great swaths of wheat
over the earth, has climbed above the crowd,
above the waves that swallowed up his child,
above even the frontiers of lament, to save
with his own soul the soul of the world:
                                    then
men untried by suffering, then women,
feeble and embittered women, who speak only
when laying out the dead or at the death-feast,
may both cry out:
                    "Harsh father, though his sun
was near its setting, still he kept his fearful course,
hoping to save his own pathetic life."
And others may exclaim:
                                    "He leaves the world,

70

leaves the settled ways of men, and goes
is search of the impossible."
                              So they may talk.
But you, great father, father of all of us
who from our earliest years have seen that everything
lies in the grave's shadow and who, with words
or chisel, have struggled with all our spirit
to rise above this flesh-consuming rhythm:
                              father,
since for us too the earth and the heavens are one
and our own thought is the world's hearth and center,
since we also say that earth may mingle with the stars
as a field's subsoil with its topsoil, so that the heavens too
may bring forth wheat:
                              father, at those times
when life's bitterness weighs with its full burden
on our hearts, and our strength can be roused no more by
        youth
but only by the Will that stands watchful
even over the grave, because to It the sea
which hugs the drowned remorselessly is itself shallow,
and shallow too the earth where the dead sleep;

in the dawn hours, as still we struggle on,
while the living and the dead both lie in the same
dreamless or dream-laden slumber, do not stop
ascending in front of us, but climb always
with slow even wings the heavens of our Thought,
eternal Daedalus, Dawnstar of the Beyond.

THE SUICIDE OF ATZESIVANO
DISCIPLE OF BUDDHA

Irreproachably Atzesivano
took up the knife, his soul
at that moment a white pigeon.
And as a star at night
glides from the sky's inmost sanctuary
or as an apple blossom falls in the gentle breeze,
so his spirit took wing from his breast.

Deaths like this are not wasted.
Because only those who love life
in its mystical first glory
can reap by themselves
the great harvest of their existence—
spent now—with a divine tranquillity.

THE SACRED WAY*

Through the new wound that fate had opened in me
I felt the setting sun flood my heart
with a force like that of water when it pours
through a hole in a sinking ship.
                                    Because again,
like one long sick when he first ventures forth
to milk life from the outside world, I walked
alone at dusk along the road that starts
at Athens and for its destination has
the sanctuary at Eleusis—the road
that for me was always the Soul's road. It bore,
like a huge river, carts slowly drawn by oxen,
loaded with sheaves or wood, and other carts
that quickly passed me by, the people in them
        shadow-like.

But farther on, as if the world
had disappeared and nature alone was left,
unbroken stillness reigned. And the rock I found
rooted at the roadside seemed like a throne
long predestined for me. And as I sat
I folded my hands over my knees, forgetting if
it was today that I'd set out or if
I'd taken this same road centuries before.

But then, rounding the nearest bend, three shadows
entered this stillness: a gypsy and, after him,
dragged by their chains, two heavy-footed bears.

And then, as they drew near to me, the gypsy,
took his tambourine down from his shoulder,
struck it with one hand, and with the other tugged

fiercely at the chains. And the two bears
rose on their hind legs heavily.
                                One of them,
the larger—clearly she was the mother—
her head adorned with tassels of blue beads
crowned by a white amulet, towered up
suddenly enormous, as if she were
the primordial image of the Great Goddess,
the Eternal Mother, sacred in her affliction,
who, in human form, was called Demeter
here at Eleusis, where she mourned her daughter,
and elsewhere, where she mourned her son,
was called Alcmene or the Holy Virgin.
And the small bear at her side, like a big toy,
like an innocent child, also rose up, submissive,
not sensing yet the years of pain ahead
or the bitterness of slavery mirrored
in the burning eyes his mother turned on him.

But because she, dead tired, was slow to dance,
the gypsy, with a single dexterous jerk
of the chain hanging from the young bear's nostril—
bloody still from the ring that had pierced it
perhaps a few days before—made the mother,
groaning with pain, abruptly straighten up
and then, her head turning toward her child,
dance vigorously.
                                And I, as I watched, was drawn
outside and far from time, free from forms
closed within time, from statues and images.
I was outside, I was beyond time.

And in front of me I saw nothing except
the large bear, with the blue beads on her head,
raised by the ring's wrench and her ill-fated tenderness,

74

huge testifying symbol
of all the world, the present and the past,
huge testifying symbol
of all primaeval suffering for which,
throughout the human centuries, the soul's
tax has still not been paid. Because the soul
has been and still is in Hell.
                              And I,
who am also slave to this world,
kept my head lowered as I threw a coin
into the tambourine.
                    Then, as the gypsy
at last went on his way, again dragging
the slow-footed bears behind him, and vanished
in the dusk, my heart prompted me once more
to take the road that terminates among
the ruins of the Soul's temple, at Eleusis.
And as I walked my heart asked in anguish:
"Will the time, the moment ever come when the bear's soul
and the gypsy's and my own, that I call initiated,
will feast together?"
                      And as I moved on, night fell,
and again through the wound that fate had opened in me
I felt the darkness flood my heart as water
pours through a hole in a sinking ship.
Yet when—as though it had been thirsting for that flood—
my heart sank down completely into the darkness,
sank completely as though to drown in the darkness,
a murmur spread through all the air above me,
a murmur,
            and it seemed to say:
                              "It will come."

LETTER IV

Hold my hand; soon we'll be rounding the cape
thundering in the distance as though a whole
world is coming apart against its rocks.
Hold my hand tightly until You feel my heartbeat
rising through Your veins into Your soul's depths,
taming the sea, its shores spread with white bones.
Hold my hand tightly and feel the god-like
premonition raising its secret wave
above all else, and do not hinder it
with words or thought, but lay Your mind on my mind
like clouds that lie the one against the other
until a flash of lightning fuses them
in a blinding dazzle and, mingled like this,
raises them instantly to their source.

Hold my hand firmly if You really long
to mount with me beyond man's bitter limits
and reach Rhythm's highest peak, the peak
of danger too, the pass of Death itself,
the source—O godly omen—from which the great
sea of freedom spreads, huge, powerful,
rolling its emeralds with its own motion towards
the ultimate pole. O don't, don't let go
of my hand, I beg You, don't let go of it.

REHEARSING FOR DEATH*

Memory has no end here and no beginning...

The fever was a crown of scarlet roses
around my forehead, a crown so tightly fixed
I could not take it off, and a holy
delirium had risen up inside me,
when You, in the shadow's sacred gateway,
in the haze where my eyelids were immersed,
half-opened the door, Your hair loose, arriving
not as a bitter mourner, all lamentation,
to weep in early spring over my body
where it lay stretched out corpse-like on my bed,
but as Astarte, who days ahead prepared
her body so that she might enter Hades with it,
might bring her body's light to Hades,
to make all Hades radiant with her body;

and serenely she reviewed the days
of her great, her god-like trial: three days
to fast, three more to wash herself completely
in the sacred springs, to wash her hair,
bring her head delight, to comb and brush it,
paint her lips; and when she'd dressed herself
in seven robes, the one over the other
slowly revolving like planets around
her divine nakedness, she would then go down
step by step into the Darkness, throwing off
a robe at each gate until, in the depths,
in the ultimate holy depths, she brought
her never-setting light to Hades
so that her nakedness would abolish Hades;

You too came down to me like this, prepared,
and lay down close to me, mute, motionless,
and Hades was abolished in my heart,
Hades became a resurrection and a triumph,
I held the great pearl in my hand, took spring
into my heart, and felt the scarlet roses
of my fever suddenly become
a crown, felt my black bed become a ship,
the unhurried ship of God, and my struggle
the navigator of my mind among the stars.

Even the Shunammite did not lie like this*
in David's bed to warm his frozen limbs,
David the prophet and king whose spirit now
no longer knew the psalms and in whose heart
was spent that holy virile heat which roused
the king and prophet in him, the fighter,
the dancer, the first defender of God's ark;
even the Shunammite did not lie down
beside David as You lay beside me
that time my heart was sinking into Hades.

Because You did not come to mingle with
the treasures of my pain from streets where mortals walk;
but as two stars circling for countless ages
mingle suddenly, the one beside the other,
and earth and heaven are full at their mating,
so You lay down beside me, and I stretched out
one hand to touch the sky and with the other
gently I held Your head, and the whole earth
filled with our embrace, the earth sailed among
the stars, the earth sang psalms, and my bed's prow
climbed toward the pole, crushing the waves of time,
and beginning, voyage, end, were all
a cataclysm of celestial light before me.

78

And there, from my being's depths, from the depths
where a god lay hidden in my mind's shadow,
the holy delirium was now set free,
and from the obscurity of my silences
powerful verses suddenly engulfed
my brain, quick verses, and they spoke these words:

"For You this bed is not a sick man's bed
but the mystical trireme of Dionysus
that flies above the waves of time, above
the closed Rhythms of Creation, flies swiftly,
like an arrow, flies with great force.

Listen to Your freedom's sound; if only now
the whole of You was burning with a fever
and if Your body flamed like pine kindling,
it was so that You could discover how to burn.
Because now You are coming near the fire
that is not in creation but in the mind
of the Creator Himself. The star that shines
beside You is Hebe's, eternal Hebe's,
the star that pierces through the light of day.

You are no longer with those things the sun illumines
but seem to be a fire-enkindled soul
in the sun's depths, You seem inside the sun,
and the flames that light the other stars, that light
the world, are now outside, outside of You.
You see the stars; the stars do not see You.
You see the world; the world does not see You.
You seem all hidden in Your passions' sun
and from there You aim Your arrows where
creation's stubbornness has not yet dawned.
For You this passion is a rehearsal for death:
rehearse it as is worthy of the holy fire

deep inside You, that Your mind encloses
not as created but as Creator.
It is a rehearsal for death, a great beginning,
height and depth are one now; Your mind is on
Olympus, Your heart gently illumines Hades.
A great beginning, a great bow has been placed
in Your hands, and do not be afraid
to bend it, so that the arrow of your longing
wings far beyond all obstacles,
until You join the living god who rises
in one resurrection after another,
striving to create one flesh above all else,
flesh out of his flesh; the living god,
striving always to shape, not in marble
or in verse, but in a deathless body,
a soul and stature worthy of his breath;
sleepless Artificer, seeking through fire
to make the clay statue of man at last
incandescent. Listen to Your freedom's sound...

Death for You is now the shape of longing:
nourish it until it rises to the height
of its deliverance, crushing death with death. *

I no longer say to You: to emerge
from the ages You must Yourself become an age.
Behind You the world burns like Troy,
and its burning is reflected deep in things past
as in the sunset the windows of a city
blaze with reflected flames, then suddenly
sink into the coming night.

And beyond—
smoke, clouds from the same fire—what man
regards as things to come dissolve slowly

and end in nothing. But You, release Yourself
continually from time. Leave the ignorant
and coarse-cut generation to its thinking:
nothing but lies and debris; plunge wholly
into the immortal shudder
that floods Your mind, where the stubbornness
of creation has not yet dawned, plunge
so that the whole radiance of Thought, the total
'Let there be...' lights up Your mind and body."

This way the God who hides deep inside me
set free for me the holy delirium
with his sudden verses, at the moment
when, like Astarte entering Hades—
even the Shunammite never entered
David's bed like that—You suddenly drew
the blood and spirit from the fever burning
my forehead, drew it into this mystical fever,
into the perfect rehearsal for death
that, piercing through the day's deception
locked until yesterday inside my heart,
now shatters the barriers of time,
breaks the barriers of fate and the world;
and enthroned above time and fate, above
the world, where the stubbornness of creation
has not yet dawned, from there releases
(O star of Youth, star of eternal Youth),
for a divinely rejuvenated universe,

(Memory has no end here and no beginning)

the oceanic sound of my freedom!

AGRAPHON*

Once at sunset Jesus and His disciples
were on their way outside the walls of Zion
when suddenly they came to where the town
for years had dumped its garbage: burnt mattresses
from sickbeds, broken pots, rags, filth.

And there, crowning the highest pile, bloated,
its legs pointing at the sky, lay a dog's carcass;
and as the crows that covered it flew off
when they heard the approaching footsteps, such a stench
rose up from it that all the disciples, hands
cupped over their nostrils, drew back as one man.

But Jesus calmly walked on by Himself
toward the pile, stood there, and then gazed
so closely at the carcass that one disciple,
not able to stop himself, called out from a distance,
"Rabbi, don't You smell that terrible stench?
How can You go on standing there?"

Jesus, His eyes fixed on the carcass,
answered: "If your breath is pure, you'll smell
the same stench inside the town behind us.
But now my soul marvels at something else,
marvels at what comes out of this corruption.
Look how that dog's teeth glitter in the sun:
like hailstones, like a lily, beyond decay,
a great pledge, mirror of the Eternal, but also
the harsh lightning-flash, the hope of Justice!"

So He spoke; and whether or not the disciples
understood His words, they followed Him
as He moved on, silent.

82

And now, Lord, I,
the very least of men, ponder Your words
and, filled with one thought, I stand before You:
grant me, as now I walk outside my Zion,
and the world from end to end is all ruins, garbage,
all unburied corpses choking the sacred
springs of breath, inside and outside the city:
grant me, Lord, as I walk through this terrible stench,
one single moment of Your holy calm,
so that I, dispassionate, may also pause
among this carrion and with my own eyes
somewhere see a token, white as hailstones,
as the lily—something glittering suddenly
deep inside me, above the putrefaction,
beyond the world's decay, like the dog's teeth
at which You gazed in wonder, Lord, that sunset:
a great pledge, mirror of the Eternal, but also
the harsh lightning-flash, the hope of Justice!

GEORGE SEFERIS

From
MYTHISTORIMA*

1

The angel—
three years we waited intently for him
closely watching
the pines the shore and the stars.
One with the plough's blade or the keel of the ship,
we were searching to rediscover the first seed
so that the primordial drama could begin again.

We returned to our homes broken,
limbs incapable, mouths cracked
by the taste of rust and brine.
When we woke we travelled towards the north, strangers
plunged into mists by the spotless wings of swans that wounded
     us.
On winter nights the strong wind from the east maddened us,
in the summers we were lost in the agony of days that couldn't
     die.

We brought back
these carved reliefs of a humble art.

3

I woke with this marble head in my hands;
it exhausts my elbows and I don't know where to put it down.
It was falling into the dream as I was coming out of the dream
so our life became one and it will be very difficult for it to
        disunite again.

I look at the eyes: neither open nor closed
I speak to the mouth which keeps trying to speak
I hold the cheeks which have broken through the skin
I don't have any more strength.

My hands disappear and come toward me
mutilated.

4

Argonauts

And if the soul
is to know itself
it must look
into a soul:*
the stranger and enemy, we've seen him in the mirror.

They were fine men, my companions, they never complained
about the work or the thirst or the frost,

they had the bearing of trees and waves
that accept the wind and the rain
accept the night and the sun
without changing in the midst of change.
They were fine men, whole days
they sweated at the oars with lowered eyes
breathing in rhythm
and their blood reddened a submissive skin.
Sometimes they sang, with lowered eyes
as we were passing the dry island with the Barbary figs
to the west, beyond the cape
of the barking dogs.
If it is to know itself, they said
it must look into a soul, they said
and the oars struck the sea's gold
in the sunset.
We went past many capes many islands the sea
leading to another sea, gulls and seals.
Sometimes unfortunate women wept
lamenting their lost children
and others raging sought Alexander the Great
and glories buried in the heart of Asia.
We moored on shores full of night-scents
with birds singing, waters that left on the hands
the memory of great happiness.
But the voyages did not end.
Their souls became one with the oars and the oarlocks
with the solemn face of the prow
with the rudder's wake
with the water that shattered their image.
The companions died one by one,
with lowered eyes. Their oars
mark the place where they sleep on the shore. *

No one remembers them. Justice.

5

We didn't know them
                it was the hope deep down that said
we'd known them since early childhood.
We saw them perhaps twice and then they took to the ships:
cargoes of coal, cargoes of grain, and our friends
lost beyond the ocean for ever.
Dawn finds us beside the tired lamp
drawing on paper, awkwardly, with effort,
ships mermaids or sea-shells;
at dusk we go down to the river
because it shows us the way to the sea;
and we spend our nights in cellars that smell of tar.

Our friends have left us
                perhaps we never saw them, perhaps
we met them when sleep
still brought us close to the breathing wave
perhaps we search for them because we search for the other life
beyond the statues.

9

The harbor is old, I can't wait any longer
for the friend who left for the island of pine trees
or the friend who left for the island of plane trees
or the friend who left for the open sea.
I stroke the rusted cannons, I stroke the oars
so that my body may revive and decide.
The sails give off only the smell
of salt from the other storm.

90

If I chose to remain alone, what I longed for
was solitude, not this kind of waiting,
my soul shattered on the horizon,
these lines, these colors, this silence.

The night's stars take me back to the anticipation
of Odysseus waiting for the dead among the asphodels.*
When we moored here among the asphodels we hoped to find
the gorge that saw Adonis wounded.

10

Our country is closed in, all mountains
that day and night have the low sky as their roof.
We have no rivers, we have no wells, we have no springs,
only a few cisterns—and these empty—that echo, and that we
        worship.
A stagnant hollow sound, the same as our loneliness
the same as our love, the same as our bodies.
We find it strange that once we were able to build
our houses, huts, and sheepfolds.
And our marriages, the cool coronals and the fingers,*
become enigmas inexplicable to our soul.
How were our children born, how did they grow strong?

Our country is closed in. The two black Symplegades*
close it in. When we go down
to the harbours on Sunday to breathe
we see, lit in the sunset,
the broken planks from voyages that never ended,
bodies that no longer know how to love.

15

Quid πλατανὼν *opacissimus?**

Sleep wrapped you in green leaves like a tree
you breathed like a tree in the quiet light
in the limpid spring I looked at your face:
eyelids closed, eyelashes brushing the water.
In the soft grass my fingers found your fingers
I held your pulse a moment
and felt your heart's pain in another place.

Under the plane tree, near the water, among laurel
sleep moved you and scattered you
around me, near me, without my being able to touch the whole
        of you—
one as you were with your silence;
seeing your shadow grow and diminish,
lose itself in the other shadows, in the other
world that let you go yet held you back.

The life that they gave us to live, we lived.
Pity those who wait with such patience
lost in the black laurel under the heavy plane trees
and those, alone, who speak to cisterns and wells
and drown in the voice's circles.
Pity the companion who shared our privation and our sweat
and plunged into the sun like a crow beyond the ruins,
without hope of enjoying our reward.

Give us, outside sleep, serenity.

16

*The name is Orestes**

On the track, on the track again, on the track,
how many times around, how many blood-stained laps, how
     many black
rows; the people who watch me,
who watched me when, in the chariot,
I raised my hand glorious, and they roared triumphantly.

The froth of the horses strikes me, when will the horses tire?
The axle creaks, the axle burns, when will the axle burst into
     flame?
When will the reins break, when will the hooves
tread flush on the ground
on the soft grass, among the poppies
where, in the spring, you picked a daisy?
They were lovely, your eyes, but you didn't know where to
     look
nor did I know where to look, I, without a country,
I who go on struggling here, how many times around?
and I feel my knees give way over the axle
over the wheels, over the wild track—
knees buckle easily when the gods so will it,
no one can escape, there's no point in being strong, you can't
escape the sea that cradled you and that you search for
at this time of trial, with the horses panting,
with the reeds that used to sing in autumn to the Lydian mode
the sea you cannot find no matter how you run
no matter how you circle past the black, bored Eumenides,
unforgiven.

22

So very much having passed before our eyes
that our eyes in the end saw nothing, but beyond
and behind was memory like the white sheet one night in an
    enclosure
where we saw strange visions, even stranger than you,
pass by and vanish into the motionless foliage of a pepper tree;

having known this fate of ours so well
wandering among broken stones, three or six thousand years
searching in collapsed buildings that might have been our
    homes
trying to remember dates and heroic deeds:
will we be able?

having been bound and scattered,
having struggled, as they said, with non-existent difficulties
lost, then finding again a road full of blind regiments,
sinking in marshes and in the lake of Marathon,
will we be able to die properly?

IN THE MANNER OF G.S.

Wherever I travel Greece wounds me.

On Pelion among the chestnut trees the Centaur's shirt*
slipped through the leaves to fold around my body
as I climbed the slope and the sea came after me
climbing too like mercury in a thermometer
till we found the mountain waters.
On Santorini touching islands that were sinking*
hearing a pipe play somewhere on the pumice stone
my hand was nailed to the gunwale
by an arrow shot suddenly
from the confines of a vanished youth.
At Mycenae I raised the great stones and the treasures of the
        house of Atreus
and slept with them at the hotel "Belle Helène de Ménélas";
they disappeared only at dawn when Cassandra crowed,
a cock hanging from her black throat.
On Spetses, Poros, and Mykonos*
the barcaroles sickened me.

What do they want, all those who say
they're in Athens or Piraeus?
Someone comes from Salamis and asks someone else whether
        he "originates from Omonia Square?"
"No, I originate from Syntagma," replies the other, pleased;*
"I met Yianni and he treated me to an ice cream."
Meanwhile Greece is travelling
and we don't know anything, we don't know we're all sailors
        out of work,
we don't know how bitter the port becomes when all the ships
        have gone;
we mock those who do know.

Strange people! they say they're in Attica but they're really
    nowhere;
they buy sugared almonds to get married
they carry hair tonic, have their photographs taken
the man I saw today sitting against a background of pigeons
    and flowers
let the hands of the old photographer smoothe away the
    wrinkles
left on his face
by all the birds in the sky.

Meanwhile Greece goes on travelling, always travelling
and if we see "the Aegean flower with corpses"*
it will be with those who tried to catch the big ship by
    swimming after it
those who got bored waiting for the ships that cannot move
the ELSI, the SAMOTHRAKI, the AMVRAKIKOS.
The ships hoot now that dusk falls on Piraeus,
hoot and hoot, but no capstan moves,
no chain gleams wet in the vanishing light,
the captain stands like a stone in white and gold.

Wherever I travel Greece wounds me,
curtains of mountains, archipelagos, naked granite.
They call the one ship that sails AGONY 937.

M/S Aulis, waiting to sail. Summer 1936

EPIPHANY, 1937

The flowering sea and the mountains in the moon's waning
the great stone close to the Barbary figs and the asphodels
the jar that refused to go dry at the end of day
and the closed bed by the cypress trees and your hair
golden; the stars of the Swan and that other star, Aldebaran.

I've kept a hold on my life, kept a hold on my life, travelling
among yellow trees in driving rain
on silent slopes loaded with beech leaves
no fire on their peaks; it's getting dark.
I've kept a hold on my life; on your left hand a line
a scar at your knee, perhaps they exist
on the sand of the past summer perhaps
they remain there where the north wind blew as I hear
an alien voice around the frozen lake.
The faces I see do not ask questions nor does the woman
bent as she walks giving her child the breast.
I climb the mountains; dark ravines; the snow-covered
plain, into the distance stretches the snow-covered plain, they
        ask nothing
neither time shut up in dumb chapels nor
hands outstretched to beg, nor the roads.
I've kept a hold on my life whispering in a boundless silence
I no longer know how to speak or how to think; whispers
like the breathing of the cypress tree that night
like the human voice of the night sea on pebbles
like the memory of your voice saying "happiness."
I close my eyes looking for the secret meeting place of the
        waters
under the ice the sea's smile, the closed wells,
groping with my veins for those veins that escape me
there where the water-lilies end, and that man

who walks blindly across the snows of silence.
I've kept a hold on my life, with him, looking for the water
    that touches you
heavy drops on green leaves, on your face
in the empty garden, drops in the motionless reservoir
striking a swan dead in its white wings,
living trees and your eyes staring.

This road has no end, has no relief, however hard you try
to recall your childhood years, those who left, those
lost in sleep, in the graves of the sea,
however much you ask bodies you've loved to stoop
under the harsh branches of the plane trees there
where a ray of the sun, naked, stood still
and a dog leapt and your heart shuddered,
the road has no relief; I've kept a hold on my life.

                                 The snow
and the water frozen in the hoofmarks of the horses.

OUR SUN

This sun was mine and yours; we shared it.
Who's suffering behind the golden silk, who's dying?
A woman beating her dry breasts cried out: "Cowards,
they've taken my children and torn them to shreds, you've
     killed them
gazing at the fire-flies at dusk with a strange look,
lost in blind thought."
The blood was drying on a hand that a tree made green,
a warrior was asleep clutching the lance that flared against his
     side.

It was ours, this sun, we saw nothing behind the gold
     embroidery
then the messengers came, dirty and breathless,
stuttering unintelligible words
twenty days and nights on the barren earth with thorns only
twenty days and nights feeling the bellies of the horses
     bleeding
and not a moment's break to drink the rain water.
You told them to rest first and then to speak, the light had
     blinded you.
They died saying: "We don't have time," touching some rays
     of the sun.
You'd forgotten that no one rests.

A woman howled "Cowards" like a dog in the night.
Once she would have been beautiful like you
with wet mouth, veins alive beneath the skin,
with love.

This sun was ours; you kept all of it, you didn't want to follow
     me.

And it was then I found out about those things behind the gold
    and the silk:
we don't have time. The messengers were right.

INTERLUDE OF JOY

That whole morning we were full of joy,
my God, how full of joy.
First, stones leaves and flowers shone
then the sun
a huge sun all thorns and so high up in the sky.
A nymph collected our cares and hung them on the trees
a forest of Judas trees.
Young loves and satyrs played there and sang
and you could see pink limbs among the black laurels
bodies of little children.
The whole morning long we were full of joy;
the abyss a closed well
tapped by the tender hoof of a young fawn.
Do you remember its laugh—how full of joy!
Then clouds rain and the wet earth.
You stopped laughing when you lay down in the hut
and opened your large eyes as you watched
the archangel practicing with a fiery sword—
"Inexplicable," you said, "inexplicable.
I don't understand people:
no matter how much they play with colors
they are all black."

                                    Penteli, spring

THE LAST DAY

The day was cloudy. No one could come to a decision;
a light wind was blowing. "Not a north-easter, the sirocco,"
     someone said.
A few slender cypresses nailed to the slope and the sea,
gray with shining pools, beyond.
The soldiers presented arms as it began to drizzle.
"Not a north-easter, the sirocco," was the only decision heard.
And yet we knew that by the following dawn
nothing would be left to us, neither the woman drinking sleep
     at our side
nor the memory that we were once men,
nothing at all by the following dawn.

"This wind reminds me of spring," said my friend
as she walked beside me gazing into the distance, "the spring
that came suddenly in winter by the closed-in sea.
So unexpected. So many years have gone. How are we going
     to die?"

A funeral march meandered through the thin rain.
How does a man die? Strange no one's thought about it.
And for those who have thought about it, it's like a
     recollection from old chronicles
from the time of the Crusades or the battle of Salamis.
Yet death is something that happens: how does a man die?
Yet each of us earns his death, his own death, which belongs
     to no one else
and this game is life.
The light was sinking over the clouded day, no one decided
     anything.

The following dawn nothing would be left to us, everything
        surrendered, even our hands,
and our women slaves at the springheads and our children
in the quarries.*
My friend, walking beside me, was singing a disjointed song:
"In spring, in summer, slaves..."
One recalled old teachers who'd left us orphans.
A couple passed, talking:
"I'm sick of the dusk, let's go home,
let's go home and turn on the light."

                                              Athens, Feb. '39

NARRATION

That man walks along weeping
no one can say why
sometimes they think he's weeping for lost loves
like those that torture us so much
on summer beaches with the gramophones.

Other people go about their business
endless paper, children growing up, women
ageing awkwardly.
He has two eyes like poppies
like cut spring poppies
and two trickles in the corners of his eyes.

He walks along the streets, never lies down
striding small squares on the earth's back
instrument of a boundless pain
that's finally lost all significance.

Some have heard him speak
to himself as he passed by
about mirrors broken years ago
about broken forms in the mirrors
that no one can ever put together again.
Others have heard him talk about sleep
images of horror on the threshold of sleep
faces unbearable in their tenderness.

We've grown used to him, he's presentable and quiet
only that he walks along weeping continually
like willows on a riverbank you see from the train
as you wake uncomfortably some clouded dawn.

We've grown used to him; like everything else you're used to
he doesn't stand for anything
and I talk to you about him because I can't find
anything that you're not used to;
I pay my respects.

LES ANGES SONT BLANCS

To Henry Miller

*Tout à coup Louis cessa de frotter ses jambes l'une contre
l'autre et dit d'une voix lente: "les anges sont blancs."*
                                                    *BALZAC**

Like a sailor in the shrouds he slipped over the tropic of
      Cancer and the tropic of Capricorn
and it was natural he couldn't stand before us at a man's
      height
but looked at us all from the height of a fire-fly or from the
      height of a pine tree
drawing his breath deeply in the dew of the stars or in the dust
      of the earth
Naked women with bronze leaves from a Barbary fig tree
      surrounded him
extinguished lamp posts airing stained bandages of the great
      city
ungainly bodies producing Centaurs and Amazons
when their hair touched the Milky Way.

And days have passed since the first moment he greeted us
      taking his head off and placing it on the iron table
while the shape of Poland changed like ink drunk by
      blotting-paper
and we journeyed among shores of islands bare like strange
      fish-bones on the sand
and the whole sky, empty and white, was a pigeon's huge wing
      beating with a rhythm of silence
and dolphins under the colored water turned dark quickly
      the soul's movements
like movements of the imagination and the hands of men who
      grope and kill themselves in sleep

106

in the huge unbroken rind of sleep that wraps around us,
  common to all of us, our common grave
with brilliant minute crystals crushed by the motion of reptiles.
And yet everything was white because the great sleep is white
  and the great death
calm and serene and isolated in an endless silence.
And the cackling of the guinea-hen at dawn and the cock that
  crowed falling into a deep well
and the fire on the mountain-side raising hands of sulphur and
  autumn leaves
and the ship with its forked shoulder-blades more tender than
  our first love-making,
all were things isolated even beyond the poem
that you abandoned when you fell heavily along with its last
  word,
knowing nothing any longer among the white eyeballs of the
  blind and the sheets
that you unfolded in fever to cover the daily procession
of people who fail to bleed even when they strike themselves
  with axes and nails;
they were things isolated, put somewhere else, and the steps of
  whitewash
descended to the threshold of the past and found silence and
  the door didn't open
and it was as if your friends, in great despair, knocked loudly
  and you were with them
but you heard nothing and dolphins rose around you dumbly in
  the seaweed.
And again you gazed intently and that man, the teeth-marks of
  the tropics in his skin,
putting on his dark glasses as if he were going to work with a
  blow-lamp, said humbly, pausing at every word:
"The angels are white flaming white and the eye that would
  confront them shrivels

and there's no other way you've got to become like stone if
  you want their company
and when you look for the miracle you've got to scatter your
  blood to the eight points of the wind
because the miracle is nowhere but circulating in the veins of
  man."

Hydra - Athens, Nov. '39

THE KING OF ASINI

and Asini . . .
ILIAD*

All morning long we looked around the citadel*
starting from the shaded side, there where the sea,
green and without lustre—breast of a slain peacock—
received us like time without an opening in it.
Veins of rock dropped down from high above,
twisted vines, naked, many-branched, coming alive
at the water's touch, while the eye following them
struggled to escape the tiresome rocking,
losing strength continually.

On the sunlit side a long empty beach
and the light striking diamonds on the huge walls.
No living thing, the wild doves gone
and the king of Asini, whom we've been trying to find for
          two years now,
unknown, forgotten by all, even by Homer,
only one word in the *Iliad* and that uncertain,
thrown here like the gold burial mask.
You touched it, remember its sound? Hollow in the light
like a dry jar in dug earth:
the same sound that our oars make in the sea.
The king of Asini a void under the mask
everywhere with us everywhere with us, under a name:
"and Asini . . . and Asini . . ."
                              and his children statues
and his desires the fluttering of birds, and the wind
in the gaps between his thoughts, and his ships
anchored in a vanished port:
under the mask a void.

Behind the large eyes the curved lips the curls
carved in relief on the gold cover of our existence
a dark spot that you see travelling like a fish
in the dawn calm of the sea:
a void everywhere with us.
And the bird that flew away last winter
with a broken wing
the shelter of life,
and the young woman who left to play
with the dog-teeth of summer
and the soul that sought the lower world squeaking
and the country like a large plane-leaf swept along by the
        torrent of the sun
with the ancient monuments and the contemporary sorrow.

And the poet lingers, looking at the stones, and asks himself
does there really exist
among these ruined lines, edges, points, hollows, and curves
does there really exist
here where one meets the path of rain, wind, and ruin
does there exist the movement of the face, shape of the
        tenderness
of those who've shrunk so strangely in our lives,
those who remained the shadow of waves and thoughts with
        the sea's boundlessness
or perhaps no, nothing is left but the weight
the nostalgia for the weight of a living existence
there where we now remain unsubstantial, bending
like the branches of a terrible willow tree heaped in
        permanent despair
while the yellow current slowly carries down rushes
        uprooted in the mud
image of a form that the sentence to everlasting bitterness
        has turned to stone:
the poet a void.

Shieldbearer, the sun climbed warring,
and from the depths of the cave a startled bat
hit the light as an arrow hits a shield:
"and Asini . . . and Asini . . ." Would that that were the king of
    Asini
we've been searching for so carefully on this acropolis
sometimes touching with our fingers his touch upon the
    stones.

Asini, summer '38 - Athens, Jan. '40

STRATIS THALASSINOS AMONG THE AGAPANTHI*

There are no asphodels, violets, or hyacinths;
how then can you talk with the dead?
The dead know the language of flowers only;
so they keep silent
they travel and keep silent, endure and keep silent,
past the country of dreams, past the country of dreams.*

If I start to sing I'll call out
and if I call out—
the agapanthi order silence
raising the tiny hand of a blue Arabian child
or even the footfalls of a goose in the air.

It's painful and difficult, the living are not enough for me
first because they do not speak, and then
because I have to ask the dead
in order to go on farther.
There's no other way: the moment I fall asleep
the companions cut the silver strings
and the flask of the winds empties.*
I fill it and it empties, I fill it and it empties;
I wake
like a goldfish swimming
in the lightning's crevices
and the wind and the flood and the human bodies
and the agapanthi nailed like the arrows of fate
to the unquenchable earth
shaken by convulsive nodding,
as if loaded on an ancient cart
jolting down gutted roads, over old cobblestones,

the agapanthi, asphodels of the negroes:
how can I grasp this religion?

The first thing God made is love
then comes blood
and the thirst for blood
roused by
the body's sperm as by salt.
The first thing God made is the long journey;
that house there is waiting
with its blue smoke
with its aged dog
waiting for the homecoming so that it can die.
But the dead must guide me;
it is the agapanthi that keep them from speaking.
like the depths of the sea or the water in a glass.
And the companions stay on in the palaces of Circe:
my dear Elpenor! My poor, foolish Elpenor!*
Or don't you see them
— "Oh help us!" —
on the blackened ridge of Psara?*

Transvaal, 14 January '42

AN OLD MAN ON THE RIVER BANK

To Nani Panayiotopoulo

And yet we should consider how we go forward.
To feel is not enough, nor to think, nor to move
nor to put your body in danger in front of an old loophole
when scalding oil and molten lead furrow the walls.

And yet we should consider towards what we go forward,
not as our pain would have it, and our hungry children
and the chasm between us and the companions calling from the
      opposite shore;
nor as the bluish light whispers it in an improvised hospital,
the pharmaceutic glimmer on the pillow of the youth operated
      on at noon;
but it should be in some other way, I would say like
the long river that emerges from the great lakes enclosed deep
      in Africa,
that was once a god and then became a road and a benefactor,
      a judge and a delta;
that is never the same, as the ancient wise men taught,
and yet always remains the same body, the same bed, and the
      same Sign,
the same orientation.

I want no more than to speak simply, to be granted that grace.
Because we've loaded even our songs with so much music that
      they're slowly sinking
and we've decorated our art so much that its features have
      been eaten away by gold
and it's time to say our few words because tomorrow our soul
      sets sail.

If pain is human we are not human beings merely to suffer
      pain;
that's why I think so much these days about the great river,
that symbol which moves forward among herbs and greenery
and beasts that graze and drink, men who sow and harvest,
great tombs even and small habitations of the dead.
That current which goes its way and which is not so different
      from the blood of men,
from the eyes of men when they look straight ahead without
      fear in their hearts,
without the daily tremor for trivialities or even for important
      things;
when they look straight ahead like the traveller who is used
      to gauging his way by the stars,
not like us, the other day, gazing at the enclosed garden of a
      sleepy Arab house,
behind the lattices the cool garden changing shape, growing
      larger and smaller,
we too changing, as we gazed, the shape of our desire and our
      hearts,
at noon's precipitation, we the patient dough of a world that
      throws us out and kneads us,
caught in the embroidered nets of a life that was as it should
      be and then became dust and sank into the sands
leaving behind it only that vague dizzying sway of a tall
      palm tree.

Cairo, 20 June '42

LAST STOP

Few are the moonlit nights that I've cared for:
the alphabet of the stars—which you spell out
as much as your fatigue at the day's end allows
and from which you gather new meaning and hope—
you can then read more clearly.
Now that I sit here, idle, and think about it, *
few are the moons that remain in my memory:
islands, color of a grieving Virgin, late in the waning
or moonlight in northern cities sometimes casting
over turbulent streets, rivers, and limbs of men
a heavy torpor.
Yet here last evening, in this our final port
where we wait for the hour of our return home to dawn
like an old debt, like money lying for years
in a miser's safe, and at last
the time for payment comes
and you hear the coins falling onto the table;
in this Etruscan village, behind the sea of Salerno
behind the harbors of our return, on the edge
of an autumn squall, the moon
outstripped the clouds, and houses
on the slope opposite became enamel:
Amica silentia lunae. *

This is a train of thought, a way
to begin to speak of things you confess
uneasily, at times when you can't hold back, to a friend
who escaped secretly and who brings
word from home and from the companions,
and you hurry to open your heart
before exile forestalls you and alters him.
We come from Arabia, Egypt, Palestine, Syria;

116

the little state
of Kommagene, which flickered out like a small lamp,
often comes to mind,
and great cities that lived for thousands of years
and then became pasture land for cattle,
fields for sugar-cane and corn.
We come from the sand of the desert, from the seas of
        Proteus,
souls shrivelled by public sins,
each holding office like a bird in its cage.
The rainy autumn in this gorge
festers the wound of each of us
or what you might term differently: nemesis, fate,
or simply bad habits, fraud and deceit, *
or even the selfish urge to reap reward from the blood of
        others.
Man frays easily in wars;
man is soft, a sheaf of grass,
lips and fingers that hunger for a white breast
eyes that half-close in the radiance of day
and feet that would run, no matter how tired,
at the slightest call of profit.
Man is soft and thirsty like grass,
insatiable like grass, his nerves roots that spread;
when the harvest comes
he would rather have the scythes whistle in some other field;
when the harvest comes
some call out to exorcise the demon
some become entangled in their riches, others deliver speeches.
But what good are exorcisms, riches, speeches
when the living are far away?
Is man ever anything else?
Isn't it this that confers life?
A time for planting, a time for harvesting.

"The same thing over and over again," you'll tell me, friend.
But the thinking of a refugee, the thinking of a prisoner, the
      thinking
of a person when he too has become a commodity—
try to change it; you can't.
Perhaps he would have liked to stay king of the cannibals
wasting strength that nobody buys,
to promenade in fields of agapanthi*
to hear the drums with bamboo overhead,
as courtiers dance with prodigious masks.
But the country they're chopping up and burning like a pine
      tree—you see it
either in the dark train, without water, the windows broken,
      night after night
or in the burning ship that according to the statistics is bound
      to sink—
this is riveted in the mind and doesn't change
this has planted images like those trees
that cast their branches in virgin forests
so that they take root in the earth and sprout again;
they cast their branches that sprout again, striding mile after
      mile;
our mind is a virgin forest of murdered friends.
And if I talk to you in fables and parables
it's because it's more gentle for you that way; and horror
really can't be talked about because it's alive,
because it's mute and goes on growing:
memory-wounding pain
drips by day drips in sleep.*

To speak of heroes to speak of heroes: Michael
who left the hospital with his wounds still open,
perhaps he was speaking of heroes—the night
he dragged his foot through the darkened city—

118

when he howled, groping over our pain: "We advance in the
    dark,
we move forward in the dark..."
Heroes move forward in the dark.

Few are the moonlit nights that I care for.

Cava dei Tirreni, 5 October '44

HELEN

TEUCER: ... *in sea-girt Cyprus, where it was decreed*
               by Apollo that I should live, giving the city
               the name of Salamis in memory of my island home.
. . . .

HELEN: *I never went to Troy; it was a phantom.*
. . . .

SERVANT: *What? You mean it was only for a cloud that we struggled*
               so much?

                                  EURIPIDES, *HELEN**

"The nightingales won't let you sleep in Platres."*

Shy nightingale, in the breathing of the leaves,
you who bestow the forest's musical coolness
on the sundered bodies, on the souls
of those who know they will not return.
Blind voice, you who grope in the darkness of memory
for footsteps and gestures—I wouldn't dare say kisses—
and the bitter raging of the slave woman grown wild.

"The nightingales won't let you sleep in Platres."

Platres: where is Platres? And this island: who knows it?
I've lived my life hearing names I've heard before:
new countries, new idiocies of men
or of the gods;
                  my fate, which wavers
between the last sword of some Ajax
and another Salamis,
brought me here, to this shore.

120

                              The moon
rose from the sea like Aphrodite,
covered the Archer's stars, now moves to find
the Heart of Scorpio, and changes everything.
Truth, where's the truth?
I too was an archer in the war;
my fate: that of a man who missed his target.

Lyric nightingale,
on a night like this, by the shore of Proteus,
the Spartan slave girls heard you and began their lament,
and among them—who would have believed it?—Helen!
She whom we hunted so many years by the banks of the
        Scamander.
She was there, at the desert's lip; I touched her; she spoke to
        me:
"It isn't true, it isn't true," she cried.
"I didn't board the blue-bowed ship.
I never went to valiant Troy."

Breasts girded high, the sun in her hair, and that stature
shadows and smiles everywhere,
on shoulders, thighs, and knees;
the skin alive, and her eyes
with the large eyelids,
she was there, on the banks of a Delta.
                              And at Troy?
At Troy, nothing: just a phantom image.
The gods wanted it so.
And Paris, Paris lay with a shadow as though it were a solid
        being;
and for ten whole years we slaughtered ourselves for Helen.

Great suffering had fallen on Greece.
So many bodies thrown

into the jaws of the sea, the jaws of the earth*
so many souls
fed to the millstones like grain.
And the rivers swelling, blood in their silt,
all for a linen undulation, a filmy cloud,
a butterfly's flicker, a wisp of swan's down,
an empty tunic—all for a Helen.
And my brother?
                    Nightingale nightingale nightingale,
what is a god? What is not a god? And what is there in
        between them?

"The nightingales won't let you sleep in Platres."

Tearful bird,
            on sea-kissed Cyprus
consecrated to remind me of my country,
I moored alone with this fable,
if it's true that it is a fable,
if it's true that mortals will not again take up
the old deceit of the gods;
                            if it's true
that in future years some other Teucer,
or some Ajax or Priam or Hecuba,
or someone unknown and nameless who nevertheless saw
a Scamander overflow with corpses,
isn't fated to hear
messengers coming to tell him
that so much suffering, so much life,
went into the abyss
all for an empty tunic, all for a Helen.

122

MEMORY I

And there was no more sea. *

And I with only a reed in my hands.
The night was deserted, the moon waning,
earth smelled of the last rain.
I whispered: memory hurts wherever you touch it,
there's only a little sky, there's no more sea,
what they kill by day they carry away in carts and dump
        behind the ridge.

My fingers were running idly over this flute
that an old shepherd gave to me because I said good
        evening to him.
The others have abolished every kind of greeting:
they wake, shave, and start the day's work of slaughter
as one prunes or operates, methodically, without passion;
sorrow's dead like Patroclus, and no one makes a mistake.

I thought of playing a tune and then I was ashamed of the
        other world
the one that watches me from beyond the night from within
        my light
woven of living bodies, naked hearts
and love that belongs to the Furies
as it belongs to man and to stone and to water and to grass
and to the animal that looks straight into the eye of its
        approaching death.

So I continued along the dark path
and turned into my garden and dug and buried the reed
and again I whispered: some morning the resurrection will
        come,

123

dawn's dew will glisten like trees in spring,
the sea will be born again, and the wave will again fling
    forth Aphrodite.
We are the seed that dies. And I entered my empty house.

MEMORY II

He spoke while sitting on what seemed to be
the marble remnant of an ancient gate;
endless the plain on the right and empty,
on the left the last shadows moved down the mountain:
"The poem is everywhere. Your voice
sometimes travels beside it
like a dolphin keeping company for a while
with a golden sloop in the sunlight,
then vanishing again. The poem is everywhere,
like the wings of the wind moved by the wind
to touch for a moment the seagull's wings.
The same as our lives yet different too,
as a woman's face changes yet remains the same
after she strips naked. He who has loved
knows this; in the light that other people see things,
the world spoils; but you remember this:
Hades and Dionysus are the same."*
He spoke and then took the main road
that leads to the old harbor, devoured now
under the rushes there. The twilight
as if ready for the death of some animal,
so naked was it.

                 I remember still:
he was traveling to Ionian shores,
to empty shells of theatres
where only the lizard slithers over the dry stones,
and I asked him: "Will they be full again some day?"
and he answered: "Maybe, at the hour of death."
And he ran across the orchestra howling

"Let me hear my brother!"
And the silence surrounding us was harsh,
leaving no trace at all on the glass of the blue.

EURIPIDES THE ATHENIAN

He grew old between the fires of Troy
and the quarries of Sicily.

He liked seashore caves and pictures of the sea.
He saw the veins of men
as a net the gods made to catch us in like wild beasts:
he tried to break through it.
He was a sour man, his friends were few;
when his time came he was torn to pieces by dogs.*

From
THREE SECRET POEMS

I:4

Years ago you said:
"Essentially I'm a matter of light."
And still today when you lean
on the broad shoulders of sleep
or even when they anchor you
to the sea's drowsy breast
you look for crannies where the blackness
has worn thin and has no resistance,
groping you search for the lance—
the lance destined to pierce your heart
and lay it open to the light.

I:7

Flame is healed by flame,
not in the slow trickle of moments
but in a single flash, at once;
like the longing that merges with another longing
so that the two remain transfixed
or like
the rhythm in music that stays
there at the center like a statue
immovable.

This breath of life is not a transition:
the thunderbolt rules it.

II:6

When will you speak again?
Our words are the children of many people.
They are sown, are born like infants,
take root, are nourished with blood.
As pine trees
hold the wind's imprint
after the wind has gone, is no longer there,
so words
retain a man's imprint
after the man has gone, is no longer there.
Perhaps the stars are trying to speak,
those that stamped your total nakedness one night—
the Swan, the Archer, the Scorpion—
perhaps those.
But where will you be the moment
the light comes, here, to this theatre?

III:14

Now
with the lead melted for divination,*
with the brilliance of the summer sea,
all life's nakedness,
the transition and the standing still, the subsidence and the
        upsurge,
the lips, the gently touched skin—
all are longing to burn.

As the pine tree at the stroke of noon
mastered by resin
strains to bring forth flame
and can't endure the pangs any longer—

summon the children to gather the ash,
to sow it.
Everything that has passed has fittingly passed.

And even what has not yet passed
must burn
this noon when the sun is riveted
to the heart of the many-petalled rose.

ODYSSEUS ELYTIS

ANNIVERSARY

I brought my life this far
To this spot which struggles
Forever near the sea
Youth upon the rocks, breast
To breast against the wind
Where is a man to go
Who is nothing other than a man
Reckoning with the coolness his green
Moments, with waters the visions
Of his hearing, with wings his remorse
O Life
Of a child who becomes a man
Forever near the sea when the sun
Teaches him to breathe there where the shadow
Of a seagull vanishes.

I brought my life this far
White addition, black total
A few trees and a few
Wet pebbles
Gentle forehead
Anticipation wept all night and is no more
Nor is anyone.
Were but a free footstep to be heard
A rested voice to rise
The poops to ripple at the jetty, inscribing
A name in darker blue upon their horizon
A few years, a few waves
Sensitive rowing
In the bays surrounding love.

I brought my life this far
Bitter furrow in the sand that will vanish
—Whoever saw two eyes touch his silence
And mixed with their sunshine, closing a thousand worlds
Let him remind his blood in other suns
Nearer the light

There is a smile that pays for the flame—
But here in the ignorant landscape that loses itself
In an open and merciless sea
Success sheds
Whirling feathers
And moments that have become attached to the earth
Hard earth under the soles of impatient feet
Earth made for vertigo
A dead volcano.

I brought my life this far
A stone pledged to the liquid element
Beyond the islands
Lower than the waves
Next to the anchors
—When keels pass, splitting with passion
Some new obstacle, and triumph over it
And hope dawns with all its dolphins
The sun's gain in a human heart—
The nets of doubt draw in
A figure in salt
Carved with effort
Indifferent, white,
Which turns towards the sea the void of its eyes
Supporting infinity.

HELEN

Summer was killed with the first drop of rain
Moistening the words that had given birth to starlight,
All those words whose single goal was You.
Where will we stretch our hands now the weather no longer takes
    us into account?
On what will we rest our eyes now the distant horizons have been
    shipwrecked by the clouds
Now that your eyelashes have closed over our landscapes
And—as though the fog passed through us—
We are left alone, utterly alone, encircled by your dead images?

Forehead to windowpane we keep watch for the new sorrow
Death will not lay us low so long as You exist
So long as there exists a wind elsewhere to enjoy you fully
To clothe you from close at hand as our hope clothes you from far
    away
So long as there exists elsewhere
A green plain reaching beyond your laughter to the sun
Telling the sun secretly how we meet again
No, it is not death we will confront
But the minutest autumnal raindrop
An obscure feeling
The smell of wet earth in our souls that grow continually
    farther apart.

And if your hand is not in our hand
If our blood is not in the veins of your dreams,
The light in the immaculate sky
And the unseen music inside us
Still bind us, sad wayfarer, to the world

It is the damp wind, the autumnal hour, the separation,
The elbow's bitter prop on the memory
That awakens when night starts to cut us off from the light
Behind the square window facing towards grief
Revealing nothing
Because it has already become unseen music, flame in the
      fireplace, chime of the huge clock on the wall
Because it has already become
A poem, line succeeding line, sound keeping pace with the rain,
      tears and words—
Words not like others but whose single goal is You.

ADOLESCENCE OF DAY

Adolescence of day, joy's springhead
The ancient myrtle waves its banner
The larks' breast will open to the light
And a song will hang suspended in mid-air
Sowing the four winds
With golden grains of fire

Liberating earth's beauty.

MARINA OF THE ROCKS

You have a taste of tempest on your lips—But where did you
    wander
All day long in the hard reverie of stone and sea?
An eagle-bearing wind stripped the hills
Stripped your longing to the bone
And the pupils of your eyes received the message of chimera
Spotting memory with foam!
Where is the familiar slope of short September
On the red earth where you played, looking down
At the broad rows of the other girls
The corners where your friends left armfuls of rosemary.

But where did you wander
All night long in the hard reverie of stone and sea?
I told you to count in the naked water its luminous days
On your back to rejoice in the dawn of things
Or again to wander on yellow plains
With a clover of light on your breast, heroine of iambics.

You have a taste of tempest on your lips
And a dress red as blood
Deep in the gold of summer
And the perfume of hyacinths—But where did you wander
Descending toward the shores, the pebbled bays?

There was cold salty seaweed there
But deeper a human feeling that bled
And you opened your arms in astonishment naming it
Climbing lightly to the clearness of the depths
Where your own starfish shone.

Listen. The word is the prudence of the aged
And time is a passionate sculptor of men
And the sun stands over it, a beast of hope
And you, closer to it, embrace a love
With a bitter taste of tempest on your lips.

It is not for you, blue to the bone, to think of another summer,
For the rivers to change their bed
And take you back to their mother
For you to kiss other cherry trees
Or ride on the north-west wind.

Propped on the rocks, without yesterday or tomorrow,
Facing the dangers of the rocks, your hair dishevelled by the
      hurricane
You will say farewell to the riddle that is yours.

THE AGE OF BLUE MEMORY

Olive trees and vineyards as far as the sea
Red fishing smacks beyond, as far as memory
August's golden sheaves in midday slumber
With seaweed and shells. And that green boat,
Just launched, still blessing the water's peaceful breast with
    "God will provide."

The years went by, leaves or pebbles,
I recall the young men, the sailors who left,
Their sails dyed the color of their hearts
Their songs telling of the four horizons
The north winds tattooed on their chests.

What was I looking for when you arrived, painted by the rising
    sun
The sea's age in your eyes
The sun's health in your body—what was I looking for
Deep in the sea-caves, in the spacious dreams
Where the wind scattered its feelings like foam
Unknown and blue, carving its sea-emblem on my chest.

Sand on my fingers, I closed my fingers
Sand on my eyes, I clasped my fingers
It was the sorrow—
I remember it was April when I first felt your human weight
Your human body, clay and sin,
Like our first day of earth
Feast-day of the amaryllis—I remember your pain:
A deep bite on the lips
A deep nail-mark on the skin where time's track is traced
    eternally.

Then I left you
And a deafening wind shook the white houses
Shook white feelings freshly washed into the sky
Radiant and smiling.

Now I will have beside me a pitcher of deathless water,
I will have a diagram of the wind's shattering freedom
And these your hands where Love will be tormented
And this your shell where the Aegean will echo.

AEGEAN MELANCHOLY

What linking of soul to the halcyons of the afternoon!
What calm in the voices of the distant shore!
The cuckoo in the trees' mantilla,
And the mystic hour of the fishermen's supper,
And the sea playing on its concertina
The long lament of the woman,
The lovely woman who bared her breasts
When memory found the cradles
And lilac sprinkled the sunset with fire.

With caique and the Virgin's sails
Sped by the winds they are gone,
Lovers of the lilies' exile;
But how night here attends on sleep
With murmuring hair on shining throats
Or on the great white shores;
And how with Orion's gold sword
Is scattered and spilled aloft
Dust from the dreams of girls
Scented with mint and basil.

At the crossroad where the ancient sorceress stood
Burning the winds with dry thyme, there,
Lightly, holding a pitcher full with the waters of silence,
Easily, as though they were entering Paradise,
Supple shadows stepped . . .
And from the crickets' prayer that fermented the fields
Lovely girls with the moon's skin have risen
To dance on the midnight threshing-floor . . .

O signs, you who pass in the depths
Of the mirror-holding water—
Seven small lilies that sparkle—

When Orion's sword returns
It will find poor bread under the lamp
But life in the stars' embers;
It will find generous hands linked in space,
Abandoned seaweed, the shore's last children,
Years, green gems . . .

O green gem—what storm-prophet saw you
Halting the light at the birth of day,
The light at the birth of the two eyes of the world.

FORM OF BOEOTIA

Here where the lonely glance blows over stone and aloe
Where time's steps sound deeply
And huge clouds unfurl their golden banners
Above the sky's metope,
Tell me from what source eternity sprang
Which is the sign that torments you
And what is the helminth's fate.

O land of Boeotia made lucid by the wind

What became of the chorus of naked hands under the palaces
Of mercy that rose like sacred smoke?
Where are the gateways with the ancient singing birds
And the uproar waking the people's terror
When the sun entered as though triumphant
When fate writhed on the heart's spear
And fratricidal murmuring caught fire?
What became of the deathless libations of March
Of the Greek lines in the undulating grass?

Foreheads and elbows have been wounded
Time rolled vermilion through the expanse of sky
Men have forged ahead
Full of pain and dreams

Acrid form: ennobled by the wind
Of a summer storm that leaves its whitehot tracks
In the lines of hills and eagles
In the lines of destiny on your palm

What can you confront, what can you wear
Dressed in the music of grass, and how do you move on

Through the heather or sage
To the arrow's ultimate mark?

On this red soil of Boeotia
Among the rocks' desolate march
You will ignite the golden sheaves of fire,
Uproot memory's evil crop,
Leave a bitter soul to the wild mint.

THE MAD POMEGRANATE TREE

Inquisitive matinal high spirits
à perdre haleine

In these all-white courtyards where the south wind blows
Whistling through vaulted arcades, tell me, is it the mad
      pomegranate tree
That leaps in the light, scattering its fruitful laughter
With windy wilfulness and whispering, tell me, is it the mad
      pomegranate tree
That quivers with foliage newly born at dawn
Raising high its colors in a shiver of triumph?

On plains where the naked girls awake,
When they harvest clover with their light brown arms
Roaming round the borders of their dreams—tell me, is it the
      mad pomegranate tree,
Unsuspecting, that puts the lights in their verdant baskets
That floods their names with the singing of birds—tell me
Is it the mad pomegranate tree that combats the cloudy skies
      of the world?

On the day that it adorns itself in jealousy with seven kinds of
      feathers,
Girding the eternal sun with a thousand blinding prisms
Tell me, is it the mad pomegranate tree
That seizes on the run a horse's mane of a hundred lashes,
Never sad and never grumbling—tell me, is it the mad
      pomegranate tree
That cries out the new hope now dawning?

Tell me, is that the mad pomegranate tree waving in the
      distance,
Fluttering a handkerchief of leaves of cool flame,

146

A sea near birth with a thousand ships and more,
With waves that a thousand times and more set out and go
To unscented shores—tell me, is it the mad pomegranate tree
That creaks the rigging aloft in the lucid air?

High as can be, with the blue bunch of grapes that flares and
    celebrates
Arrogant, full of danger—tell me, is it the mad pomegranate
    tree
That shatters with light the demon's tempests in the middle of
    the world
That spreads far as can be the saffron ruffle of day
Richly embroidered with scattered songs—tell me, is it the mad
    pomegranate tree
That hastily unfastens the silk apparel of day?

In petticoats of April the first and cicadas of the feast of mid-
    August
Tell me, that which plays, that which rages, that which can
    entice
Shaking out of threats their evil black darkness
Spilling in the sun's embrace intoxicating birds
Tell me, that which opens its wings on the breast of things
On the breast of our deepest dreams, is that the mad
    pomegranate tree?

I NO LONGER KNOW THE NIGHT

I no longer know the night, death's terrible anonymity
A fleet of stars has dropped anchor in the depths of my soul
Hesperus, sentinel, so that you may shine
Close to the heavenly breeze of an island that dreams of me
Announcing the dawn from its high crags
My two eyes, embracing you, steer you by the star
Of my true heart: I no longer know the night.

I no longer know the names of the world that denies me
With clarity I read the shells, the leaves, the stars
Vain is my antagonism on the sky's highroads
Unless it is the dream that gazes at me again
With tears as I cross the sea of deathlessness
Hesperus, beneath the arc of your golden fire
The night that is only night I now no longer know.

148

BODY OF SUMMER

A long time has passed since the last rain was heard
Above the ants and lizards
Now the sun burns endlessly
The fruit paints its mouth
The pores in the earth open slowly
And beside the water that drips in syllables
A huge plant gazes into the eye of the sun.

Who is he that lies on the shores beyond
Stretched on his back, smoking silver-burnt olive leaves?
Cicadas grow warm in his ears
Ants are at work on his chest
Lizards slide in the grass of his arm pits
And over the seaweed of his feet a wave rolls lightly
Sent by the little siren that sang:

"O body of summer, naked, burnt
Eaten away by oil and salt
Body of rock and shudder of the heart
Great ruffling wind in the osier hair
Breath of basil above the curly pubic mound
Full of stars and pine needles
Body, deep vessel of the day!

"Soft rains come, violent hail
The land passes lashed in the claws of a snowstorm
Which darkens in the depths with furious waves
The hills plunge into the dense udders of the clouds
And yet behind all this you laugh carefree
And find your deathless moment again
As the sun finds you again on the sandy shores
As the sky finds you again in your naked health."

BURNISHED DAY, CONCH OF THE VOICE...

Burnished day, conch of the voice that fashioned me
Naked, to step through my perpetual Sundays
Between the shores' cries of welcome,
Let your wind, known for the first time, blow freely
Unfold a lawn of tenderness
Where the sun can roll his head
Can enflame the poppies with his kiss
Poppies nourished by men so fine
That the sole mark on their bare chests
Is the blood of defiance that annuls sorrow
And attains the remembrance of liberty.

I spoke of love, of the rose's health, of the ray
That by itself goes straight to the heart,
Of Greece that steps so surely on the sea
Greece that carries me always
Among naked snow-crowned mountains.

I give my hand to justice
Diaphanous fountain, sublimest spring,
My sky is deep and changeless
All I love is incessantly reborn
All I love is always at its beginning.

DRINKING THE SUN OF CORINTH

Drinking the sun of Corinth
Reading the marble ruins
Striding across vineyards and seas
Sighting along the harpoon
A votive fish that slips away
I found the leaves that the sun's psalm memorizes
The living land that passion joys in opening.

I drink water, cut fruit,
Thrust my hand into the wind's foliage
The lemon trees water the summer pollen
The green birds tear my dreams
I leave with a glance
A wide glance in which the world is recreated
Beautiful from the beginning to the dimensions of the heart!

I LIVED THE BELOVED NAME

I lived the beloved name
In the shade of the aged olive tree
In the roaring of the lifelong sea

Those who stoned me live no longer
With their stones I built a fountain
To its brink green girls come
Their lips descend from the dawn
Their hair unwinds far into the future

Swallows come, infants of the wind
They drink, they fly, so that life goes on
The threat of the dream becomes a dream
Pain rounds the good cape
No voice is lost in the breast of the sky

O deathless sea, tell me what you are whispering
I reach your morning mouth early
On the peak where your love appears
I see the will of the night spilling stars
The will of the day nipping the earth's shoots

I sow a thousand wild lilies on the meadows of life
A thousand children in the true wind
Beautiful strong children who breathe out kindness
And know how to gaze at the horizons
When music raises the islands

I carved the beloved name
In the shade of the aged olive tree
In the roaring of the lifelong sea.

THIS WIND THAT LOITERS

This wind that loiters among the quinces
This insect that sucks the vines
This stone that the scorpion wears next to his skin
And these sheaves on the threshing-floor
That play the giant to small barefoot children.

The images of the Resurrection
On walls that the pine trees scratched with their fingers
This whitewash that carries the noonday on its back
And the cicadas, the cicadas in the ears of the trees.

Great summer of chalk
Great summer of cork
The red sails slanting in gusts of wind
On the sea-floor white creatures, sponges
Accordions of the rocks
Perch from the fingers even of bad fishermen
Proud reefs on the fishing lines of the sun.

No one will tell our fate, and that is that.
We ourselves will tell the sun's fate, and that is that.

ALL DAY LONG WE WALKED IN THE FIELDS

All day long we walked in the fields
With our women, suns, and dogs
We played, sang, drank water
Fresh as it sprang from the ages.

In the afternoon we sat for a moment
And we looked deeply into each other's eyes
A butterfly flew from our hearts
It was whiter
Than the small branch at the tip of our dreams
We knew that it was never to disappear
That it did not remember at all what worms it bore.

At night we lit a fire
And round about it sang:

Fire, lovely fire, do not pity the logs
Fire, lovely fire, do not turn to ash
Fire, lovely fire, burn us, tell us of life.

We tell of life, we take it by the hands
We look into its eyes and it returns our look
And if this which makes us drunk is a magnet, we know it
And if this which gives us pain is bad, we have felt it
We tell of life, we go ahead
And say farewell to its birds, which are migrating.

We are of a good generation.

154

WITH WHAT STONES, WHAT BLOOD, AND WHAT IRON

With what stones, what blood, and what iron
With what fire are we made
Though we seem pure mist
And they stone us and say
That we walk with our heads in the clouds
How we pass our days and nights
God only knows.

My friend, when night wakens your electric grief
I see the tree of the heart spreading
Your arms open beneath a pure Idea
To which you call
But which will not descend
For years and years:
It up there, and you down here.

And yet longing's vision awakens flesh one day
And there where only bare solitude once shone
A city now laughs lovely as you would have it
You almost see it, it is waiting for you
Give me your hand so that we may go there before the Dawn
Floods it with cries of triumph.

Give me your hand—before birds gather
On the shoulders of men to announce in song
That Virginal Hope is seen coming at last
Out of the distant sea.

We will go together, and let them stone us
And let them say we walk with our heads in the clouds—
Those who have never felt, my friend,

With what iron, what stones, what blood, what fire
We build, dream, and sing.

From
HEROIC AND ELEGIAC SONG FOR THE LOST SECOND LIEUTENANT OF THE ALBANIAN CAMPAIGN

1

There where the sun first dwelt
Where time opened like a virgin's eyes
As the wind snowed flakes of almond blossom
And horsemen lit up the tips of the grass

There where the hoof of a gallant plane tree beat
And high up a banner waved to earth and water
Where no back ever bent under a gun's weight
But all the sky's labor,
All the world, shone like a waterdrop
In early morning, at the mountain's foot

Now, as though God were sighing, a shadow lengthens

Now agony stoops and with bony hands
Plucks and crushes the flowers one by one;
In gullies where the water has stopped flowing
Songs die from the dearth of joy;
Rocks like monks with chill hair
Cut the bread of wilderness in silence.

Winter penetrates to the mind. Something evil
Will strike. Hair of the horse-mountain bristles.

High overhead vultures share out the sky's crumbs.

3

For those men night was a more bitter day
They melted iron, chewed the earth
Their God smelled of gunpowder and mule-hide.

Each thunderclap was a death riding the sky
Each thunderclap a man smiling in the face
Of death—let fate say what she will.

Suddenly the moment misfired and struck courage
Hurled splinters head-on into the sun
Binoculars, sights, mortars, froze with terror.

Easily, like calico that the wind rips
Easily, like lungs that stones have punctured
The helmet rolled to the left side...

For one moment only roots shook in the soil
Then the smoke dissolved and the day tried timidly
To beguile the infernal tumult.

But night rose up like a spurned viper
Death paused one second on the brink—
Then struck deeply with his pallid claws.

4

Now with a still wind in his quiet hair
A twig of forgetfulness at his left ear
He lies on the scorched cape
Like a garden the birds have suddenly deserted
Like a song gagged in the darkness

Like an angel's watch that has stopped
Eyelashes barely whispered goodbye
And bewilderment became rigid...

He lies on the scorched cape
Black ages round him
Bay at the terrible silence with dog's skeletons
And hours that have once more turned into stone pigeons
Listen attentively.
But laughter is burnt, earth has grown deaf,
No one heard that last, that final cry
The whole world emptied with that very last cry.

Beneath the five cedars
Without other candles
He lies on the scorched cape.
The helmet is empty, the blood full of dirt,
At his side the arm half shot away
And between the eyebrows—
Small bitter spring, finger-print of fate
Small bitter red-black spring
Spring where memory freezes.

6

He was a fine young man. The first day he was born
The mountains of Thrace bent down to show
The wheat rejoicing on the land's shoulders.
The mountains of Thrace bent down to spit
First on his head, then on his chest, then into his tears.*
Greeks with formidable arms appeared
And raised him in swaddling-bands of the north...
Then days sped by, they hurled stones in sport

Gambolled astride fillies.
Then the early Strymons* rolled down
Till gypsy anemones everywhere rang their bells
And from earth's confines came
Sea-shepherds driving flocks of seal
To where a cave breathed deeply
To where a huge rock sighed.

He was a strong young man.
Nights lying with girls of the orange-grove
He stained the stars' great raiment,
The love inside him was such
That he drank all the earth's taste in wine,
Then danced with the white brides
Till dawn heard and spilt light into his hair,
Dawn that with open arms found him
Scratching the sun in the saddle of two small branches,
Painting the flowers,
Or with tenderness lulling
The small sleepless owls...
Ah, what strong thyme his breath,
What a proud map his naked chest
Where freedom, where the sea resounded...

He was a brave young man.
With his gold buttons and his pistol
With a man's air in his stride
And his helmet a shining target
(His brain, that had never known evil,
Was penetrated so easily)
With his soldiers on his right and left
And the avenging of injustice in front of him
—Fire against lawless fire!—
With the blood above his eyebrows
The mountains of Albania thundered

160

Then they melted snow to wash
His body, dawn's silent shipwreck
And his hands, open spaces of solitude
The mountains of Albania thundered
They did not weep
Why should they weep?
He was a brave young man.

8

Now that his fatherland has darkened on earth
Tell the sun to find another course
If he wants to save his pride.
Or with soil and water
Let him cast a small sister Greece in blue elsewhere.
Tell the sun to find another course
So as not to confront even a single daisy
Tell the daisy to flower with a new virginity
So that she will not be sullied by alien fingers.

Release the wild pigeons from the fingers
And let no sound speak of the water's suffering
As the sky blows softly into an empty shell
Send no signal of despair to any place
But bring from the gardens of chivalry
Roses where his soul stirred
Roses where his breath played
On a small nymphic chrysalis
That changes its dress as often as satin its sheen
In the sun, as the may-bugs grow drunk on gold-dust
And birds fly swiftly to learn from the trees
Through the germination of what seed this famous world was
    born.

Sun, bronze voice, and holy etesian wind
Swore on his breast to give him life
There was no room for any darker strength
Only with light spilt from the laurel branch
And silver from dew, only there the cross
Flashed, as magnanimity dawned
And kindness, sword in hand, rose up
To proclaim through his eyes and their banners "I live."

Your health, old river, you who see at dawn
Such a child of God, a twig of pomegranate
Between his teeth, perfuming himself in your waters;
Your health, village medler tree, you who preen yourself
When Androutsos* tries to steal his dreams;
And yours, noonday spring, you who touched his feet
And yours too, girl, you who were his Helen,
His little bird, his Holy Virgin, his Pleiades,
Because if only once in a lifetime
Love of a human being was to reverberate, igniting
Star after star, the secret firmaments,
The divine voice would reign always everywhere
Adorning the woods with the tiny hearts of birds
Adorning poets' words with lyres of jasmin.

And let it harrow hidden evil wherever it is to be found—
With fire let it harrow hidden evil wherever it is to be found.

13

In the distance crystal bells ring out

They speak of him who was burnt in life
As a bee in the thyme's ferment;
Of dawn choked in earthen breasts
Though it promised a brilliant day;
Of the snowflake that flashed in the mind and went out
When a distant shot was heard
And high overhead the Albanian partridge flew away
        lamenting.

They speak of him who had no time even to weep
For the deep sadness of the love of life
He had when the wind grew strong in the distance
And birds croaked on the beams of a ruined mill
For women who drank wild music
Standing at the window clasping their kerchiefs tightly
For women who drove despair to despair
Waiting for a black signal at the meadow's edge.
Then clanging horseshoes beyond the threshold
Speak of his warm, unfondled head
Of his large eyes where life had penetrated
So deeply that it could never come out again.

BEAUTY AND THE ILLITERATE

Often, at the Dormition of Twilight, her soul took on a certain
    lightness from the mountains opposite, though the day
    had been cruel and tomorrow was unknown.

Yet, when darkness came and the hand of the priest appeared
    over the garden of the dead, She,

Alone, Erect, with the few familiar companions of night—the
    rosemary breeze and the charcoal smoke from
    chimneys—lay awake on the threshold of the sea

Singularly beautiful.

Words half-formed of waves or half-guessed in a rustling, and
    others seemingly of the dead, words startled among the
    cypresses, like strange Zodiacs circling her head,
    suddenly illumined her. And an

Unbelievable clarity allowed the true landscape to appear at a
    great depth within her,

Where, beside the river, black men fought the Angel, showing
    in what manner Beauty is born.

Or what in other terms we call tears.

And as long as her thought lasted, you felt that it overflowed
    her shining face, with the bitterness in the eyes, and the
    cheekbones—like those of an ancient temple-servant—
    enormous,

Stretching from the tip of Canis Major to the tip of Virgo.

"And I, far from the pestilence of the city, imagined a desert
at her side, where tears would have no meaning and
where the only light would be that of the fire which
devoured all my possessions.

The two of us shoulder to shoulder would sustain the weight of
the future, sworn to utter silence and to a condominion
of the stars

As though I did know, illiterate as I am, that it is exactly there,
in utter silence, where the most appalling noises are
heard,

And that loneliness, from the time it became unendurable to
the heart of man, has scattered and sown stars!"

THE AUTOPSY

And so they found that the gold of the olive-root had dripped
     into the recesses of his heart.

And from the many times that he had lain awake by
     candlelight waiting for the dawn, a strange heat had
     seized his entrails.

A little below the skin, the blue line of the horizon sharply
     painted. And ample traces of blue throughout his blood.

The cries of birds which he had come to memorize in hours of
     great loneliness apparently spilled out all at once, so that
     it was impossible for the knife to enter deeply.

Probably the intention sufficed for the evil

Which he met—it is obvious—in the terrifying posture of the
     innocent. His eyes open, proud, the whole forest moving
     still on the unblemished retina.

Nothing in the brain but a dead echo of the sky.

Only in the hollow of his left ear some light fine sand, as
     though in a shell. Which means that often he had walked
     by the sea alone, with the pain of love and the roar of
     the wind.

As for those particles of fire on his groin, they show that he
     moved time hours ahead whenever he embraced a
     woman.

We shall have early fruit this year.

166

THE SLEEP OF THE BRAVE

They still smell of incense, and their faces are burnt by their
    crossing through the Great Dark Places.

There where they were suddenly flung by the Immovable

Face-down, on ground whose smallest anemone would suffice
    to turn the air of Hades bitter

(One arm outstretched, as though straining to be grasped by
    the future, the other arm under the desolate head, turned
    on its side,

As though to see for the last time, in the eyes of a
    disembowelled horse, the heap of smoking ruins) —

There time released them. One wing, the redder of the two,
    covered the world, while the other, delicate, already
    moved through space,

No wrinkle or pang of conscience, but at a great depth

The old immemorial blood that began painfully to etch, in the
    sky's blackness,

A new sun, not yet ripe,

That couldn't manage to dislodge the hoarfrost of lambs from
    live clover, but, before even casting a ray, could divine
    the oracles of Erebus... *

And from the beginning, Valleys, Mountains, Trees, Rivers,

A creation made of vindicated feelings now shone, identical
 and reversed, there for them to cross now, with the
 Executioner inside them put to death,

Villagers of the limitless blue!

Neither twelve o'clock striking in the depths nor the voice of
 the pole falling from the heights retracted their footsteps.

They read the world greedily with eyes now open forever,
 there where they were suddenly flung by the Immovable,

Face-down, and where the vultures swooped upon them to
 enjoy the clay of their guts and their blood.

LACONIC

Longing for death so scorched me that my brightness returned
to the sun.

Who now sends me into the perfect syntax of stone and air,

So he whom I sought, I am.

O flaxen summer, discreet autumn,

Most humble winter,

Life contributes its mite, the leaf of the olive tree,

And with a small cricket in the night of stupidities once more
vindicates the claim of the Unexpected.

NIKOS GATSOS

AMORGOS

To a Green Star

"The eyes and ears are bad witnesses
for men with barbarian souls"
Heraclitus
(Diels, *Die Fragm. der Vorsokr.*, B. 107)

I

With their country bound to the sails and their oars hung on
the wind
The shipwrecked voyagers slept tamely like dead beasts in
sheets of sponge
But the seaweed's eyes are turned to the sea
In case the South Wind brings them back with their lateen rigs
freshly dyed,
For a single lost elephant is always worth more than the two
moving breasts of a girl,
Only in the mountains let the roofs of deserted chapels light up
at the whim of the evening star,
Let the birds flutter in the masts of the lemon tree
With the steady white beat of a new tempo;
And then the winds will come, bodies of swans that remained
spotless, tender, motionless
Among the steam-rollers of the shops, cyclones of the
vegetable gardens,
When women's eyes turned into coal and the hearts of the
chestnut vendors broke,
When the harvesting stopped and the hopes of the cricket
began.
And that is why, my brave lads, with wine, kisses and leaves
on your lips,

That is why I would have you enter the rivers naked
And sing of the Barbary Coast as the woodman seeks out the
        mastic tree,
As the viper slithers through fields of barley,
Her proud eyes all anger,
As lightning threshes youth.

And don't laugh and don't weep and don't rejoice
Don't tighten your boots uselessly as though planting plane
        trees
Don't become FATED
Because the golden eagle is not a closed drawer,
Nor a plum-tree's tear, nor a water-lily's smile,
Nor a dove's vest, nor a sultan's mandolin,
Nor a silk kerchief for the head of a whale.
It is a marine saw carving gulls,
It is the carpenter's pillow, the beggar's watch,
It is fire in a smithy mocking the priests' wives and lulling the
        lilies to sleep,
It is the Turks' in-laws, the Australians' feast,
The Hungarians' mountain refuge
Where the hazel trees meet secretly in autumn:
They see the wise storks dying their eggs black
And then they too weep
They burn their nightgowns and wear the duck's petticoat
They spread stars on the ground for kings to tread on
With their silver amulets, the crown, the purple,
They scatter rosemary on garden beds
So the mice can cross to another cellar
And enter other churches to devour the sacred altars,
And the owls, my lads,
The owls are hooting
And dead nuns are rising to dance
With tambourines, drums and violins, with bagpipes and lutes,
With banners and censers, with herbs and magic veils,

With the bear's breeches in the frozen valley,
They eat the martens' mushrooms
They play heads and tails for St. John's ring and the Black
      Man's florins *
They ridicule the witches
They cut off a priest's beard with the cutlass of Kolokotróni *
They wash themselves in the smoke of incense,
And then, chanting slowly, they enter the earth again and are
      silent
As waves are silent, as the cuckoo at daybreak, as the
      lamplight at evening.

So in a deep jar the grape withers, and in the bell-tower of a
      fig tree the apple turns yellow
So, wearing a gaudy tie,
Summer breathes in the tent of a vine arbor
So, naked among the white cherry trees, sleeps my young love,
A girl unfading as an almond branch,
Her head resting on her elbow, her palm on her golden florin,
On its morning warmth, when, silent as a thief,
Through the window of spring the dawn star enters to wake
      her.

II

They say the mountains tremble and the fir trees rage
When night gnaws the tile-pins to let in the Kallikantzari*
When hell gulps down the torrents' foaming toil
Or when the groomed hair of the pepper tree becomes the
    North Wind's plaything.

Only Achaean cattle graze vigorous and strong
On abundant fields in Thessaly beneath an ageless, watching
    sun
They eat green grass and celery, leaves of the poplar tree, they
    drink clear water in the troughs
They smell the sweat of the earth and then fall heavily to sleep
    in the shade of the willow tree.

Cast out the dead said Heraclitus, yet he saw the sky turn pale,
Saw two small cyclamens kissing in the mud
And as the wolf comes down from the forests to see the dog's
    carcass and weep
He too fell to kiss his own dead body on the hospitable soil.
What good to me the bead that glistens on your forehead?
I know the lightning wrote its name upon your lips
I know an eagle built its nest within your eyes
But here on this damp bank there is one way only
One deceptive way and you must take it
You must plunge into blood before time forestalls you
Cross over opposite to find your companions again
Flowers birds deer
To find another sea, another tenderness,
To take Achilles' horses by the reins
Instead of sitting dumb scolding the river
Stoning the river like the mother of Kitso*

176

Because you too will be lost and your beauty will have aged.
I see your childhood shirt drying on the branches of a willow
Take it, this flag of life, to shroud your death
And may your heart not fail you
And may your tear not fall upon this pitiless earth
As a penguin's tear once fell in the frozen wilderness
Complaint achieves nothing
Life everywhere will be the same
With the serpent's flute in the land of phantoms
With the song of brigands in aromatic groves
With the knife of some sorrow in the cheek of hope
With the pain of some spring in the screech owl's heart—
Enough if a sharp sickle and plough are found in a joyful hand
Enough if there flower only
A little wheat for festivals, a little wine for remembrance, a
      little water for the dust . . .

III

In the griever's courtyard no sun rises
Only worms appear to mock the stars
Only horses sprout upon the ant hills
And bats eat birds and piss out sperm.

In the griever's courtyard night never sets
Only the foliage vomits forth a river of tears
When the devil passes by to mount the dogs
And the crows swim in a well of blood.

In the griever's courtyard the eye has gone dry
The brain has frozen and the heart turned to stone
Frog-flesh hangs from the spider's teeth
Hungry locusts scream at the vampires' feet.

In the griever's courtyard black grass grows
Only one night in May did a breeze pass through
A step light as a tremor on the meadow
A kiss of the foam-trimmed sea.

And should you thirst for water, we will wring a cloud
And should you hunger for bread, we will slaughter a
      nightingale
Only wait a moment for the wild rue to open
For the black sky to flash, the mullein to flower.

But it was a breeze that vanished, a lark that disappeared
It was the face of May, the moon's whiteness
A step light as a tremor on the meadow
A kiss of the foam-trimmed sea.

IV

Wake up limpid water from the root of the pine tree so that
you can find the sparrows' eyes and give them new life, wa-
tering the earth with scent of basil and the lizard's whistling. I
know you are a naked vein under the menacing gaze of the
wind, a voiceless spark in the luminous multitude of the stars.
No one notices you, no one stops to listen to your breathing,
but you, your pace heavy in the arrogant ranks of nature, will

one day reach the leaves of the apricot tree, will one day climb the slender bodies of young broom shrubs, will fall from the eyes of the beloved like an adolescent moon. There is a death-less stone on which a passing human angel once inscribed his name and a song that no one yet knows, not even the craziest children or the wisest nightingales. It is now locked up in a cave of Mount Devi, in the gorges and ravines of my father-land, but someday when it breaks out and thrusts itself against destruction and time, this angelic song, the rain will suddenly stop and the mud dry up, the snows will melt in the mountains, the wind will sing like a bird, the swallows will come to life, the willows will shiver, and the men of cold eyes and pallid faces—when they hear the bells tolling of their own accord in the cracked belltowers—will find festive hats to wear and gaudy bows to decorate their shoes. Because then no one will joke any longer, the blood of the brooks will overflow, the animals will break their bridles in the mangers, the hay will turn green in the stables, between the roof-tiles fresh poppies will sprout, and May flowers, and at all crossroads red fires will rise at midnight. Then slowly the frightened young girls will come to cast their last clothing into the fire and dance all naked around it, just as in our day, when we too were young, and a window would open at dawn to show a flaming carnation growing on their breasts. Lads, maybe the memory of ancestors is deeper consolation and more precious company than a hand-ful of rose water, and the intoxication of beauty no different from the sleeping rose bush of the Eurotas. So now goodnight; I see a galaxy of falling stars rocking your dreams, but I hold in my fingers music for a better day. Travellers from India have more to tell you than the Byzantine chroniclers.

V

Man, during the course of this mysterious life,
Bequeathed his descendants tokens varied and worthy of his
      immortal origin,
As he bequeathed also traces of the ruins of twilight,
      snowdrifts of celestial reptiles, diamonds, kites, and the
      glances of hyacinths,
In the midst of sighs, tears, hunger, wailing, and the ashes of
      subterranean wells.

VI

How very much I loved you only I know
I who once touched you with the eyes of the Pleiades,
Embraced you with the moon's mane, and we danced on the
      meadows of summer
On the harvest's stubble, and together ate cut clover,
Great dark sea with so many pebbles round your neck, so
      many colored jewels in your hair.

A ship nears shore, a rusted water-wheel groans.
A tuft of blue smoke in the rose of the horizon
Is like a crane's wing palpitating.
Armies of swallows are waiting to offer the brave their
      welcome
Arms rise naked, anchors engraved on the armpits
Children's cries mingle with the song of the West Wind
Bees come and go in the cows' nostrils
Kalamata* kerchiefs flutter

180

And a distant bell painting the sky with bluing
Is like the sound of a gong travelling among the stars—
A gong that escaped so many ages ago
From the souls of Goths and the domes of Baltimore*
And from lost Saint Sophia, the great cathedral.
But up in the high mountains who are they who now gaze
      down, eyes calm, faces serene?
Of what conflagration is this cloud of dust the echo?
Is Kalyvas fighting now, or is it Leventoyannis?*
Have the Germans begun to battle the noble men of Mani?*
Kalyvas isn't fighing, nor is Leventoyannis
Nor have the Germans begun to battle the noble men of Mani.
Silent towers guard a ghostly princess
The tips of cypress trees consort with a dead anemone
Shepherds unperturbed pipe their morning song on a linden
      reed
A stupid hunter fires a shot at the turtledoves
And an old windmill, forgotten by all,
Mends by itself its rotten sails with a needle of dolphin bone
And descends the slopes with a brisk northwester leading it
As Adonis descended the paths of Mount Chelmos to bid the
      lovesick shepherdess* good evening.

For years and years, O my tormented heart, have I struggled
      with ink and hammer,
With gold and fire, to fashion an embroidery for you,
The hyacinth of an orange tree,
A flowering quince tree to comfort you—
I who once touched you with the eyes of the Pleiades,
Embraced you with the moon's mane, and we danced on the
      meadows of summer
On the harvest's stubble, and together ate cut clover,
Great dark loneliness with so many pebbles round your neck,
      so many colored jewels in your hair.

DEATH AND THE KNIGHT (1513)*

As I behold you motionless
journeying through the ages with the steed of Acritas and the
      lance of Saint George,*
I could place near you,
with these dark forms that will assist you always,
until one day you too will vanish with them forever,
until you become a fire again in the great womb of Fate that
      gave you birth,
I could place near you
a bitter orange tree in the snow-covered meadows of the
      moon,
could unfold before you the veil of some evening,
with the red star of Scorpio singing of youth
with the River of Heaven spilling into August
with the North Star weeping and freezing,
I could place pastures,
streams that once watered the lilies of Germany,
and this armor that you wear, I could adorn it
with a basil-shoot and a spray of mint
with the weapons of Plapoutas and Nikitaras' trophies.*
But I who saw your descendants like birds
tear the sky of my country one spring dawn,
saw the cypresses of Morea hush
there on the plain of Nauplia,
before the ready embrace of the wounded sea,
where the centuries have fought with the crosses of courage,
I will now place near you
the embittered eyes of a child,
the closed eyelids
in the mud and blood of Holland.

This black land
will grow green some day.
The iron hand of Goetz will overturn the carts,*
will load them with sheaves of barley and rye,
and in the dark forests with their dead loves
there where time turned a virgin leaf to stone,
on breasts where a tearful rose trembled lightly
a silent star will shine like a spring daisy.

But you will stay motionless;
with the steèd of Acritas and the lance of Saint George
you will journey through the ages,
a restless hunter from the generation of heroes,
with these dark forms that will assist you always,
until one day you too will vanish with them forever,
until you become a fire again in the great womb of Fate that
        gave you birth,
until again in the river caves resound
heavy hammers of patience
not for rings and swords
but for pruning-knives and ploughs.

FOUR SONGS

The Black Sun

The sun is black, is black today,
unreal is the clear sky,
but I sat where the sea comes in
to this world of sin
and I sent the sins to their graves
in forty waves.

Luckless friend, to you I bore
freedom's lily-flower,
I gathered up with bitterness
your holy dress,
I washed it, and away the blood glides
in forty tides.

The sun is black, is black today,
and no bells play,
but I knelt on the slopes of pain
to the holy Virgin,
and wept for the victims death consumes
in forty tombs.

The Myrtle Tree

A sea in my mind,
a garden of love,
I set my sails
for the world above.

184

At the wide windows
a myrtle tree smiled;
weary of walking
I ask like a child:

Help me to find,
O myrtle most blessed,
water and earth
for the lovebirds' nest.

At the wide windows
the myrtle tree cries
as I set my sails
for paradise.

We Who are Left

We who are left on this stony ground
will burn bitter incense for the dead,
and when Charon the wrestler, new prey found,
has packed up his caravan and fled,
we'll dance in their memory round and round.

We who are left will begin each day
with a fresh-cut slice of the sun's rich bread—
golden honeycomb on a golden tray—
and now untouched by the sickle of dread
we'll steer our life forward on its way.

We who are left will scatter one dawn
seeds of grass on the desert's face,
and before night cuts us down like corn
we'll make the earth into a holy place,
a cradle for children still unborn.

Evening at Colonos

Often I walked the roads round Colonos
before autumn came, before summer went,
as the sun sank low and the day grew dark,
to tame my wild thoughts and my heart's lament.

No honeysuckle blossomed, no nightingale sang,
no Antigone led blind Oedipus by the hand,
but behind the closed windows where the rebels hid
I saw a boy studying the sages' wonderland.

He looked at the Dog Star, at Vega beyond,
at the smile of Alpha, at Omega's thorn,
he saw hills greening in the deep abyss
and love dance with death round the gates of horn.

Boy with the magic eyes among your ancient books
descrying above time the stars' horoscope,
give me, too, a glance, tell me where to find
a flickering of light, a glimmering of hope.

NOTES AND INDEX

NOTES TO POEMS

p. 3. The title is taken from Dante's *Inferno*, III, 60, and means "Who made... the great refusal."

p. 4. Achilles and Demophon did not become immortal because Achilles' father, Peleus, king of Phthia, and Demophon's mother, Metaneira, queen of Eleusis, respectively prevented the sea-goddess Thetis and the earth-goddess Demeter from completing the fire ritual that would render the two babies invulnerable and immortal.

p. 6. In 480 B.C., under the Spartan king Leonidas, the Greek forces halted the advance of the invading Persian army—the Medes—at the pass of Thermopylae. Ephialtis was the Greek traitor who guided a detachment of the Medes over a mountain path in order to attack the Greeks from the rear.

p. 10. Priam and Hecuba were king and queen of Troy during the Trojan war.

p. 12. Nero was the son of Domitius Aenobarbus and Agrippina Junior. Agrippina later married the Emperor Claudius, poisoned him, and gave the throne to her son. Nero subsequently killed his mother. The *Lares Familliares* were minor Roman deities protecting the household; little statues of them were placed by the hearth.

p. 14. A satrapy was a province governed by a satrap under the ancient Persian monarchy. Artaxerxes was probably the first of three Persian kings of that name (464-424 B.C.); Susa was the capital of the Achaemenid dynasty of Persia.

p. 15. A soothsayer had warned Julius Caesar to beware of the Ides of March, the fifteenth day of that month. On March 15, 44 B.C., the sophist Artemidoros vainly tried to hand Caesar a message disclosing the murderous plot of Brutus and Casius.

p. 16. The title is a quotation from Plutarch's *Life of Antony*, par. 75.

p. 18. The Laistrygonians and the Cyclops were cannibal giants encountered by Odysseus on his homeward journey to Ithaka.

p. 20. Zagros was the name of a range of mountains dividing Media from Assyria and Susiana, in Asia Minor; Phraata was a city of Media, winter home of the Parthian kings.

p. 21. The regal début of Cleopatra's children was organized by Antony in 34 B.C. Alexander and Ptolemaios were Antony's sons, whereas Kaisarion was the son of Julius Caesar.

p. 24. The period in which this poem is set appears to be the 9th century, shortly after the murder of the Byzantine emperor Michael III by his co-emperor Basil I, founder of the Macedonian dynasty. The "Panopolitan" of line 17 is of course the Egyptian-Greek poet Nonnus (5th c. A.D.) mentioned in line 15.

p. 25. Theodotos of Chios, a rhetorician, persuaded the Egyptians to kill Pompey (48 B.C.) when he landed in Egypt as a fugitive, after having been defeated by Julius Caesar at Pharsalus.

p. 28. There were several Hellenistic cities called Selefkia. The most splendid was Selefkia on Tigris, founded c. 312 B.C. by Selefkos I Nicator as the capital of his empire.

p. 30. Kaisarion was the son of Julius Caesar and Cleopatra. In 34 B.C. Antony conferred on him the title "King of Kings" (see "Alexandrian Kings"). After Antony's defeat, he was put to death by Augustus on the advice of his counsellors who, paraphrasing a line from the *Iliad* (II, 204), remarked: "It is not good to have too many Caesars ..."

p. 34. Dareios I (521-486 B.C.) was, after Cyrus the Great, the greatest of the Achaemenid kings of Persia, though in European history he is chiefly known for the defeat of his invading force by the Greeks at Marathon in 490 B.C. Mithridatis VI Evpator, "The Good Father," was the semi-Hellenized Persian king of Pontos (120-63 B.C.). Cicero designated him the greatest of all kings after Alexander and the most formidable opponent that the Roman army of his day encountered. He was finally defeated by Pompey in 66 B.C.

p. 36. Ammonios Sakkas, the "Socrates of Neoplatonism," taught in Alexandria and is said to have had Longinus, Herennius, Plotinus, and the two Origens among his disciples.

p. 39. The King of Sparta, Kleomenis III (235-219 B.C.), had asked Ptolemy III to help him in his war against the Macedonians and the Achaean League. Ptolemy agreed on the condition that Kleomenis' own mother, Kratisikleia, and his children be sent to Alexandria as hostages. Compared to the kings of Sparta, who claimed to be descended from Heracles, the Ptolemies, whose dynasty dated from 300 B.C., were mere upstarts.

p. 44. The Serapeion was the famous temple of Serapis in Alexandria built by Ptolemy I Sotir around 300 B.C. and destroyed by the Emperor Theodosius in A.D. 392.

p. 46. Kakergetis, "Malefactor," was the nickname of Ptolemy VIII Evergetis (170-116 B.C.). Zabinas, Grypos, and Hyrkanos, mentioned later in the poem, had rival interests in the throne of Syria.

p. 48. This opening line quotes from the inscription which Alexander the Great wrote to accompany the booty he sent to Athens from his conquests in Persia. Granikos, Issus, and Arbela were the three battles that decided the success of Alexander's Persian campaign.

190

p. 50.   Vavylas, Bishop of Antioch (237-250) and martyr, had been buried in the precinct of the famous temple of Apollo, in the grove of Daphni. The priests of Apollo abandoned the temple, which they considered to have been polluted by this burial, and the Christians built a church over Vavylas' tomb. When Julian arrived in Antioch he ordered the church to be demolished and Vavylas' relic to be carried away. The temple and statue of Apollo were destroyed on November 22, 362, by a fire which was attributed to the vengeance of the Christians.

p. 55.   Cf. Plutarch, *Life of Lycurgus*, xv, 6-7: "After giving marriage such traits of reserve and decorum, he none the less freed men from the empty and womanish passion of jealous possession, by making it honourable for them, while keeping the marriage relation free from all wanton irregularities, to share with other worthy men in the begetting of children, laughing to scorn those who regard such common privileges as intolerable, and resort to murder and war rather than grant them. For example, an elderly man with a young wife, if he looked with favour and esteem on some fair and noble young man, might introduce him to her, and adopt her offspring by such a noble father as his own." Trans. Bernadotte Perrin, *Plutarch's Lives* (London, 1928) vol. I, pp. 251-53.

p. 57.   Acrocorinth is the name of the steep and solitary mountain (1,900 feet in height) that served as the citadel of ancient Corinth.

p. 57.   Pegasus, the winged horse who ascended to the seat of the immortals and carried thunder and lightning for Zeus, was associated with Corinth and often represented on the coins of this city-state.

p. 58.   Salona is the popular name for the town of Amfissa, whose port is Itea, on the Corinthian Gulf.

p. 61.   Salamis is an island in the Saronic Gulf, visible from the mainland.

p. 61.   Kineta is a beach on the Saronic Gulf between Eleusis and Corinth. It is now a tourist center but was beautifully tree-lined and virtually deserted at the time the poem was written.

p. 63.   Thalero is a village on the Corinthian Gulf near to which Sikelianos once lived.

p. 66.   Boccaccio narrates a related dream by Dante's mother in his *Life of Dante*, xvii. He recounts that the mother gave birth to her son under a lofty laurel tree, and her son, feeding on laurel berries from this tree and drinking water from a clear spring nearby, grew to become a great shepherd. Reaching for a leafy laurel branch the son appeared to fall, and Dante's mother suddenly seemed to see not him but a peacock. The marvel of this transformation woke her. Boccaccio goes on to offer his interpretation of the dream.

p. 69.   Daedalus was the mythical figure under whose name the

Athenians and Cretans personified the earliest development of the arts of sculpture and architecture. Among Daedalus' works were the wooden cow that concealed Pasiphaë, the labyrinth at Knossos that contained the Minotaur, and the wings that brought his son Icarus to tragedy but allowed Daedalus to escape the wrath of Minos and fly free to Sicily.

p. 73.   The Sacred Way is the ancient road by which the great Iakchos procession went from Athens to Eleusis for the celebration of the Eleusinian Mysteries.

p. 77.   The title is taken from Plato's *Phaedo* (see 67e and 80d-81a).

p. 78.   David and the Shunammite (termed Shulamite by Sikelianos) appear in 1 Kings 1:1-4: "Now king David was old and stricken in years; and they covered him with clothes, but he gat no heat. Wherefore his servants said unto him, Let there be sought for my lord the king a young virgin: and let her stand before the king, and let her cherish him, and let her lie in the bosom, that my lord the king may get heat. So they sought for a fair damsel throughout all the coasts of Israel, and found Abishag a Shunammite, and brought her to the king. And the damsel was very fair, and cherished the king, and ministered to him: but the king knew her not."

p. 80.   The phrase "crushing death with death" is taken from the resurrection hymn sung on Easter Sunday in the Greek Orthodox Church.

p. 82.   The term agraphon, literally "unwritten thing," designates a saying or tradition about Christ either not recorded in the Gospels or incapable of being traced to its original source. A related parable is used by the Persian poet Nizami (1141-1203) and was adapted by Goethe for inclusion in his "Noten und Abhandlungen" appended to *West-Östlicher Divan*.

p. 87.   The colloquial meaning of the title is "novel," but it has other connotations also, as the poet indicates in the following note: "Mythistorima—it is its two components that made me choose the title of this work: Mythos, because I have used, clearly enough, a certain mythology; Istoria [both "history" and "story"], because I have tried to express, with some coherence, circumstances that are as independent from myself as the characters in a novel."

p. 88.   Aeschylus, *The Libation Bearers*, 491. Orestes is speaking at Agamemnon's tomb, reminding his father of the bath where he was slain by Clytemnestra.

p. 88.   The quotation is from Plato, *Alcibiades*, 133 B. The words are spoken by Socrates to Alcibiades.

p. 89.   See Homer, *Odyssey* xi, 75 ff., where the shade of Elpenor, youngest of Odysseus' companions, asks that his oar be planted on his seashore grave to perpetuate his memory.

192

p. 91.   In Homeric mythology the meadow of asphodels is the dwelling place of the dead.

p. 91.   During the wedding ceremony in the Orthodox Church, the bridal pair exchange both coronals and rings.

p. 91.   The Symplegades, through which Jason and the Argonauts had to pass, were dangerous clashing rocks at the juncture of the Bosphorus and the Black Sea.

p. 92.   Pliny, *Letters*, I, 3.

p. 93.   Sophocles, *Electra*, 694, from the passage which describes Orestes' participation in the chariot-races at Delphi.

p. 95.   Pelion is a mountain range in Thessalian Magnesia. The centaur, Chiron, is said to have dwelt on its wooded slopes.

p. 95.   The volcanic island of Santorini, once the center of a very ancient religion, is geologically composed of pumice stone and china clay; in her bay islands have appeared and disappeared.

p. 95.   Spetses, Poros and Mykonos are popular Aegean islands.

p. 95.   Omonia ("harmony") and Syntagma ("constitution") are the two largest squares of central Athens.

p. 96.   Aeschylus, *Agamemnon*, 659.

p. 103.   The allusion is to the *Iliad*, vi. 457: "Then in Argos . . . you shall bear water from Messeïs or Hypereia." The line is from Hector's speech to Andromache. See Thucydides, VII, 87: "At first the Syracusans treated them terribly in the stone quarries . . ." The relevant passage refers to the Athenians and their allies who were taken prisoner by the Syracusans after the destruction of the Athenian expedition to Sicily in 413 B.C.

p. 106.   From Balzac's novel *Louis Lambert*.

p. 109.   The citadel is the ruined acropolis of Asini, close to the modern village of Tolos on the coast of the Argolid. The landscape has changed considerably since the poem was written.

p. 112.   Agapanthi (literally "love flowers") are African lilies. Stratis Thalassinos means "Stratis the Mariner," a persona that appears frequently in Seferis' poetry.

p. 112.   See *Odyssey*, xxiv, 12 ff.

p. 112.   See *Odyssey*, x.

p. 113.   Elpenor, to whom reference has been made in *Mythistorima*, is a central figure in Seferis' poetry. In Homer's *Odyssey* he is described as a somewhat foolish and feeble-hearted companion who finally kills himself in a fall from Circe's palace while heavy with sleep and wine.

p. 113.   This line is from Solomos' "The Destruction of Psara" which is among the well known poems of modern Greece. The island of Psara was razed and its people massacred in 1825 during the Greek War of

Independence.

p. 116.   The phrase is from the Introduction to the *Memoirs* of General Makriyannis, one of the principal leaders of the Greek War of Independence. His *Memoirs* is, perhaps, the most important prose work in Greek literature of the nineteenth century.

p. 116.   Virgil, *Aeneid*, ii. 55.

p. 117.   Makriyannis, *Memoirs*, II, 258.

p. 118.   See first note to p. 112.

p. 118.   Aeschylus, *Agamemnon*, 179-80.

p. 120.   Euripides' play assumes that not Helen herself but a phantom of Helen went with Paris to Troy. Helen herself was carried by Hermes to the Egyptian court of Proteus, where she was eventually reunited with her husband Menelaos long after the end of the Trojan war.

p. 120.   Platres is a summer resort on the slopes of Mount Troödos in Cyprus.

p. 122.   The phrase is taken from a fresco in a countryside church at Asinou in Cyprus.

p. 123.   Revelations, 21, 1.

p. 125.   See Heracleitos, Diels *Die Fragmente der Vorsokratiker*, B. 15.

p. 127.   Euripides is said to have been killed by hunting dogs while staying at the court of Archelaus, king of Macedonia.

p. 129.   A traditional method of divination was to drop molten lead into water and read the shape taken by the cooled lead. It was practiced in modern Greece on the feast day of St. John (June 24) by unmarried girls to learn the trade or profession of their future husbands.

p. 159.   In the Orthodox baptismal ceremony, the child being baptized is spat on three times in the part of the service concerned with the expulsion of the devil.

p. 160.   The Strymon is a Thracian river.

p. 162.   Androutsos was one of the most renowned and high spirited generals of the Greek War of Independence.

p. 167.   Erebus is a place of nether darkness between earth and Hades.

p. 175.   The Black Man is the "Arapis" of Greek folk literature who emerges at night to feed his flocks gold pieces.

p. 175.   Theodoros Kolokotronis was one of the principal heroes of the Greek War of Independence.

p. 176.   The "Kallikantzari" are gross, bestial, destructive creatures who appear at night during the twelve days after Christmas.

p. 176.   Kitso was a Greek chieftain who fought against the Turks. He was captured and was about to be hanged when his mother tried to join him from the opposite bank of an impassable river. In a popular ballad she is pictured as rebuking the river, throwing stones at it and pleading with it to let her cross over to her son.

p. 180.   Kalamata is a town in the southern Peloponnesus, noted for its olives and for its multicolored silk kerchiefs.

p. 181.   Baltimore: an allusion to Edgar Allan Poe's "The Bells."

p. 181.   Kalyvas and Leventoyannis were both heroes of the Greek War of Independence, in which both were killed.

p. 181.   Mani is the rocky southern part of the middle peninsula of the Peloponnesus, legendary because the Turks were unable to occupy it on account of the bravery of its inhabitants.

p. 181.   The lovesick shepherdess is Golfo, the heroine of the nineteenth century play of small dramatic merit although still popular, written by Spiridon Persiadis. Golfo lives in a village on Mount Chelmos near Patras; she is driven mad by the loss of her lover.

p. 182.   The title and some of the imagery of this poem were suggested by Dürer's famous copperplate engraving, "The Knight, Death, and the Devil" (1513).

p. 182.   Acritas is the warrior hero of the Byzantine epic, *Digenis Acritas*.

p. 182.   Plapoutas and Nikitaras, heroes of the Greek War of Independence, were renowned for feats of great individual courage.

p. 183.   Goetz von Berlichingen was a German knight whose right hand was shot away in 1505 while he was assisting Albert IV, Duke of Bavaria, at the siege of Landshut; he substituted an iron arm and became known as "Goetz with the iron hand." Goethe made him the hero of his play, "Goetz von Berlichingen" (1771).

195

BIOGRAPHICAL NOTES

CONSTANTINE P. CAVAFY was born in Alexandria, Egypt, in 1863, the ninth and last child of Constantinopolitan parents. His father, Peter, with his brother founded and ran Cavafy Brothers, an export-import firm that prospered for several years dealing mainly in textiles between England and Egypt. Peter died in 1870, leaving the family poorly provided for, and two years later his widow took the family to England where her eldest son became manager of the family firm in London and the second son manager in Liverpool. Their inexperience resulted in the loss of the family fortunes, and in 1879 the family returned to a life of genteel poverty in Alexandria. But the seven years in England were important in the shaping of Cavafy's poetic sensibility; he became completely fluent in English and familiar with English manners, and the influence of both remained with him throughout his life. His first verse was written in English and his subsequent practice as a poet shows a substantial familiarity with the English poetic tradition. After several years without a permanent job, during which time he spent three influential years with his mother and family in Constantinople, at the age of twenty-nine Cavafy took up an appointment as special clerk in the Irrigation Service of the Ministry of Public Works in Alexandria, an appointment which he held for the next thirty years, retiring in 1922 with the rank of Assistant Director. He continued to live in Alexandria until his death, from cancer of the larynx, in 1933. Generally speaking, the poet had a rather limited circle of friends. He lived with his mother until her death in 1899, then with his unmarried brothers, and for most of his mature years alone—although he did maintain several influential literary relationships during his later years, including one with E.M. Forster who introduced his work to the *literati* of England. During his lifetime Cavafy never offered a volume of his poems for sale; his method of distributing his work was to give friends and relatives the several pamphlets of his poems that he had printed privately and a folder of his latest offprints or broadsheets. His poetry was virtually unknown and unrecognized in Greece until some time after his death.

ANGELOS SIKELIANOS was born on the Ionian island of Lefkada in 1884, the youngest of seven children. His family was a prominent one of the island and was on terms of friendship with the well-known Lefkadian poet Aristotle Valaoritis. After completing his schooling in Lefkada the poet enrolled in the Law School of Athens University, but abandoned his studies after two years and joined a theatre group, as did his sisters Penelope and Helen. At this time Penelope met and eventually married Raymond Duncan, brother of Isadora Duncan, and it was at Penelope Duncan's home in Athens that Sikelianos met Eva Palmer of New York who became his first wife and lifelong supporter. In 1909 a son, Glafkos, was born to Eva (Sikelianos' only child). During the next years Sikelianos travelled extensively in Greece, as well as to Italy, France and Palestine, and began at this time to publish prolifically, which he continued to do throughout much of his life. In the 1920's Sikelianos and Eva together attempted to organize an International Delphic Center and a Delphic University, projects that were to occupy them more or less continually for over ten years and that were ultimately unsuccessful. These projects crystallized in the Delphic Festival which took place in 1927, and again in 1930, with theatrical and dance productions, athletic games and craft exhibitions. In order to defray expenses Eva drew on her inheritance and Sikelianos mortgaged his house. In 1933 Eva returned to America. Although she continued to promote the "Delphic Idea" there and also to send some funds to her husband, she did not return to Greece until the year after his death, in 1952 (she died that year and was buried at Delphi). The years following the failure of the Delphic Idea were ones of disillusion for Sikelianos; the poet became more and more isolated and his financial situation remained insecure at best, but it was during this period that he began to develop his mature, tragic voice. In 1938 Sikelianos met Anna Karamanou, the woman who was to become his second wife; they were married in 1940, appropriately enough at Eleusis, by the altar known as the "Unlaughing Stone" where Demeter once sat to weep the loss of her daughter Persephone. In the difficult period of the German occupation of Greece and the civil war that followed, the couple lived in an apartment in Athens and in these years Sikelianos' health began to deteriorate. In 1950 he suffered a stroke. He died the following year, having mistakenly drunk a disinfectant—lysol—instead of his medicine.

GEORGE SEFERIS was born in Smyrna, in Asia Minor, in 1900, the son of a lawyer-poet. When the First World War broke out, the family moved to Athens where he completed his secondary education. In 1918 he accompanied his mother to Paris to join his father, who was working there as a lawyer. For six years he studied law in Paris, where he took his degree, and after a long visit to England in 1925 returned to Athens, where the following year he was appointed to the Greek Ministry of Foreign Affairs. His diplomatic career took him to London and Albania, and during World War II to Crete, South Africa, Egypt, London and Italy. In 1941 he married Maria Zannou. After various appointments in the Diplomatic

Service in the post-war years, he was finally appointed Greek ambassador to London, 1957-62. He retired to Athens in 1962. From the time Seferis published his first volume of poetry, *Strophe*, in 1931, which marked a turning point in modern Greek poetry, he made an outstanding contribution to Greek literature, not only as an original poet but also as a translator (notably of Eliot) and essayist. In 1963 he was awarded the Nobel Prize for Literature, and he was given honorary Doctor of Letters degrees by the universities of Cambridge, Oxford, and Princeton. He was elected an Honorary Foreign Member of the American Academy of Arts and Sciences, spent the autumn of 1968 as a member of the Institute for Advanced Study at Princeton, and read his poetry at several institutions and universities in the United States. He died in Athens in 1971, his last years clouded by the Greek military dictatorship, under which he refused to publish any new poetry.

ODYSSEUS ELYTIS was born in Crete in 1911 into a well-known industrial family that originally came from Lesbos. The family moved to Athens in 1914, and Elytis has maintained a residence there since. He was educated in Athenian secondary schools and at the University of Athens, where he studied law but did not take a degree. In 1935 he published his first poems in *Ta Nea Grammata* (The New Letters), the periodical that became the principal outlet for the so-called "generation of the Thirties," which included George Seferis, Andreas Embirikos, and several other poets who, along with Elytis, were responsible for introducing French surrealism into Greek poetry. Elytis also began to create collages at this time, an interest that reasserted itself some thirty years later, under the 1967-74 dictatorship. In 1940-41, the poet served as a Second Lieutenant in the First Army Corps during the Albanian Campaign against the invading Italian forces. During the post-war years, Elytis devoted himself almost exclusively to his writing, with two brief periods of public service as Director of Programing for the National Broadcasting Institute of Athens and a term as President of the Governing Board of the Greek Ballet. In 1960 his long poem *Axion Esti* was awarded the National Prize for Poetry, and he was subsequently decorated with the Order of the Phoenix. From 1948 to 1952 and again from 1969 to 1971, he lived in France. In the early 1960's he visited both the United Stated and Russia, and since receiving the Nobel Prize in 1979, he has travelled extensively in Europe.

NIKOS GATSOS was born in a village in Arcadia in 1914. Some years later his family moved to Athens and there he completed his secondary education, subsequently studying philology at the University of Athens. During 1935-36 he spent several months in Paris and southern France.

198

After the war Gatsos worked for the *Anglo-Greek Review,* edited by George Katsimbalis (Henry Miller's "Colossus of Maroussi") and for the National Broadcasting System. As well as writing his own poetry, Gatsos has made a number of translations, including plays by Tennessee Williams, Strindberg, Genet, and Lorca, which have been produced in Greek theatres. In recent years he has become well-known as a writer of lyrics for Greece's popular composers, notably Hadzidakis, Theodorakis, and Xahakos. Many of these songs are of great beauty and clarity and have helped to introduce distinction into Greek popular music. Over the years Gatsos has established himself as a unique literary personality in Greece. Making his venue various Athenian cafés, he has been a figure around which have gathered intellectuals and men of letters, both foreign and Greek, attracted by his inimitable presence. In his "salon," poets and writers have often had their first audience, and many have benefited from his firm but gentle guidance, not least of all foreign writers and scholars first approaching the Greek literary world.

INDEX OF FIRST LINES

THE LOCKERT LIBRARY OF POETRY
IN TRANSLATION

George Seferis: Collected Poems (1924-1955), translated, edited, and introduced by Edmund Keeley and Philip Sherrard

Collected Poems of Lucio Piccolo, translated and edited by Brian Swann and Ruth Feldman

C. P. Cavafy: Collected Poems, translated by Edmund Keeley and Philip Sherrard and edited by George Savidis

Benny Andersen: Selected Poems, translated by Alexander Taylor

Selected Poetry of Andrea Zanzotto, translated and edited by Ruth Feldman and Brian Swann

Poems of René Char, translated by Mary Ann Caws and Jonathan Griffin

Selected Poems of Tudor Arghezi, translated and edited by Michel Impey and Brian Swann

Tadeus Rózewiczi The Survivor, translated and introduced by Magnus J. Krynski and Robert A. Maguire

"Harsh World" and Other Poems by Angel González, translated by Donald D. Wash

Dante's "Rime," translated and introduced by Patrick S. Diehl

Ritsos in Parentheses, translations and introduction by Edmund Keeley

Salamander: Selected Poems of Robert Marteau, translated and introduced by Anne Winters

Angelos Sikelianos: Selected Poems, translated and introduced by Edmund Keeley and Philip Sherrard

Selected Later Poems of Marie Luise Kaschnitz, translated by Lisel Mueller

Osip Mandelstam's "Stone," translated and introduced by Robert Tracy